ROCKINGHAM COUNTY:
A BRIEF HISTORY

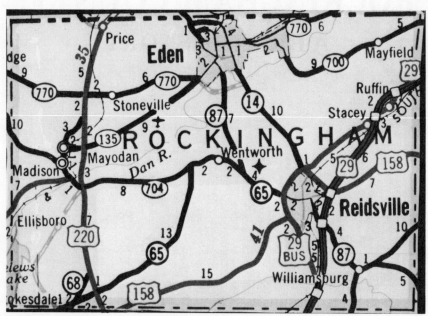

Adapted from Official Highway Map of North Carolina, 1981-1982, prepared by North Carolina Department of Transportation, Raleigh.

ROCKINGHAM COUNTY:

A BRIEF HISTORY

By Lindley S. Butler

Raleigh
North Carolina Department of Cultural Resources
Division of Archives and History
1982

DEPARTMENT OF CULTURAL RESOURCES

Sara W. Hodgkins
Secretary

DIVISION OF ARCHIVES AND HISTORY

William S. Price, Jr.
Director

Suellen M. Hoy
Assistant Director

NORTH CAROLINA HISTORICAL COMMISSION

Mrs. Frank A. Daniels, Jr.
Chairman

T. Harry Gatton
Vice-Chairman

For Tom and Will

CONTENTS

MAPS AND ILLUSTRATIONS

FOREWORD

The Division of Archives and History is fortunate to have engaged Lindley S. Butler, historian-in-residence at Rockingham Community College in Wentworth, to write *Rockingham County: A Brief History*. Dr. Butler, a native of the county, holds a doctorate from the University of North Carolina at Chapel Hill and has taught history at various colleges and universities in the state since 1963. He is a frequent contributor to historical journals and has been cited for his outstanding contributions in the field of local history. He is the author of *Our Proud Heritage: A Pictorial History of Rockingham County, N.C.* (1971) and other publications and is the editor of the *Journal of Rockingham County History and Genealogy*, published semiannually since 1976.

Rockingham County: A Brief History is the ninth in a series of county history surveys published since 1963 by the Division of Archives and History, North Carolina Department of Cultural Resources. (Additional counties treated are Bertie, Burke, Dare, Davie, Edgecombe, Lenoir, New Hanover, and Rowan.)

The manuscript was edited and seen through the press by Robert M. Topkins, historical publications editor, who also obtained some of the illustrations used in the pamphlet. Patricia R. Johnson, a member of the staff of the Historical Publications Section, proofread the publication. Funding was made possible by a special legislative appropriation.

Memory F. Mitchell
Historical Publications Administrator

April 7, 1982

INTRODUCTION

Aerial views of Rockingham County reveal the characteristic natural features and the effects of man's sojourn upon the land. A forest of old-field pine and hardwood covers over half of the low hills. Much of the cleared land is cultivated, especially in the river valleys and creek bottoms. The numerous streams and rivers are clearly visible, with the Dan River being a particularly prominent landmark. The tobacco factory, the textile complexes, and the giant brewery reflect the progress made in industrial development. Finally, the relatively small cities and towns are indicative of an evenly distributed population.

To the thoughtful observer questions arise. What, if anything, is special about this county? Is there anything unique or different about the land and the people there? What is representative of the historical experience of this county? Can a study of the county's past help to explain why its citizens think and act the way they do? The following narrative will address these and other questions and, it is hoped, give readers a better understanding of the land, the people, and the heritage of Rockingham County. A study of this scope is merely a beginning, but it may lead others to explore the county's history to the extent it deserves.

There are too many people who have contributed to my study to mention here; however, I wish to thank the many students in my county history courses who have raised questions and brought new information to light. Robert W. Carter, Jr., read the manuscript and made helpful suggestions and corrections that I greatly appreciate. I especially wish to thank my wife T, who typed this manuscript and has always offered able editorial assistance in all of my research. Only she knows how much all of my published work is a joint effort.

I. NATURAL HISTORY

The Land and Its Resources

Rockingham County lies in the northern Piedmont, adjacent to the state of Virginia. It is rectangular in shape, measuring about 46 kilometers (29 miles) east to west and 32 kilometers (20 miles) north to south. The total area of the county is 1,480 square kilometers (572 square miles) or 148,200 hectares (366,080 acres). The terrain is characteristic of the Piedmont, varying from gently rolling in the east to sharply rolling in the west. The highest elevation, 312 meters (1,022 feet), occurs at Price in the northwest; the lowest elevation, 146 meters (480 feet), occurs on the Dan River in the northeast. In a sketch of the county written in 1810, Alexander Sneed noted that "The Country is rather broken than level, tho' not mountaineous, with a Salubrious air, which renders it as healthy, perhaps, as any part of North Carolina. . . ."

The county is bisected by the Dan River, a stream 340 kilometers (210 miles) in length that rises in Virginia, flows southward into North Carolina, then returns to Virginia to join the Staunton and form the Roanoke River. The Dan, the county's most prominent geologic feature, meanders diagonally some 60 kilometers (40 miles) across the county from southwest to northeast. The Dan River watershed, which encompasses the northern two thirds of the county, is also drained by two major tributaries—the Smith and Mayo rivers—and by numerous picturesque creeks: Wolf Island, Lower and Upper Hogans, Lick Fork, Cascade, Buffalo, Matrimony, Jacobs, Rockhouse, Fall, and Beaver Island. The Dan valley, which in some places is 8 kilometers (5 miles) wide, is bordered on the south by a ridge that averages 260 meters (850 feet) in height and on the north by a low range of hills that culminates in Cedar Point Mountain, with an elevation of 303 meters (995 feet), on the Mayo River opposite the site of the old village of Avalon. There are many low falls and cascades on the streams in the watershed, the most beautiful of which are the Mayo Falls of the Mayo River, which provides excellent whitewater recreation, and, in the same area, the Fall Creek Falls.

The Haw River and its two principal tributaries, the Big and Little Troublesome creeks, enter the southern part of the county on the Guilford County line. There are no natural lakes in the county, but many farm ponds have been constructed. Belews Lake, a steam-generation impoundment constructed by Duke Power Company, has an area of 1,564 hectares (3,863 acres) and covers portions of four counties. Near the city of Reidsville are Lake Reidsville, with an area of 280 hectares (700 acres), and the smaller Lake Hunt, with an area of 63 hectares (155 acres), both of which furnish water for the city. These man-made lakes provide excellent fishing and boating recreation for the county.

With the exception of a large swamp on Lower Hogans Creek on the eastern border of the county and some sections of the Haw River, the river and creek bottoms are generally well drained and composed of a dark, sandy loam, the most fertile soil in the county. The area soils are chiefly Cecil clay loam and sandy loam and vary in color from red to yellow to gray.

The climate of the region is moderate. The temperature averages 15.4 degrees C (59.7 degrees F), and the average annual rainfall is 111.4 centimeters (43.86 inches). The growing season lasts for more than 200 days. Most winters are accompanied by several snowfalls, with an occasional heavy fall of 36 centimeters (14 inches) or more.

Natural disasters are virtually unknown to the area, although floods on the Dan River and windstorms have occurred infrequently. For the most part, residents of the county have wisely refrained from either commercial or residential construction on the floodplains, and non-agricultural flood damage is relatively light. The most extensive flood in recent years occurred in 1972 as a result of heavy rains generated by Hurricane Agnes. At least two meteorites have fallen in the county during the period of recorded history. The first, which fell at Deep Springs in 1846, measured 11,500 grams (25.4 pounds) and is currently held by the North Carolina Museum of Natural History in Raleigh. The Smith's Mountain meteorite, discovered in 1866, originally weighed 5,000 grams (11 pounds). Portions of it are in the state natural history museum and at museums in Paris, London, and Vienna.

A wide range of flora and fauna abounds in Rockingham County. A forest of mixed hardwood and old-field pine covers more than half the county and shelters a variety of birds and small animals. Numerous species of songbirds, as well as the Great Blue Heron, the Little Green Heron, wild ducks and geese, kingfishers, cranes, and other water birds, live on the county's rivers and ponds. Wildlife is abundant. Among the more commonly seen species are rabbits, squirrels, opossums, skunks, groundhogs, beavers, raccoons, and foxes. Deer are plentiful throughout the county, although the largest concentrations are found in lowlands along rivers. In recent years an occasional black bear has been sighted, probably a wanderer from neighboring Caswell County.

Many varieties of ferns and wild flowers grow in the forests, especially on the stream banks. From early spring to late fall, flowering plants embellish the woods, fields, and roadsides with color and a special beauty. The more spectacular wild flowers common to the area are several species of orchid, azalea, laurel, and rhododendron.

At present only a few of the county's natural areas are being preserved. Following an unsuccessful effort to establish a state park, James G. W. MacLamroc of Greensboro in 1978 donated his property at

Troublesome Creek Ironworks and High Rock Ford on the Haw River to the Conservation Foundation of North Carolina. At the present time there are no plans to develop these areas. In 1980, following a successful public campaign to raise funds for an endowment, the Spray Water Power and Land Company donated to the trustees of Rockingham Community College the 4-hectare (10-acre) Bear Slide Natural Area on the Smith River in Eden. The area, rich in wild flowers, includes a floodplain and bluffs overlooking the river. It is open to the public for guided tours. Other publicly owned natural areas are Camp Saurakee, a county-owned 32-hectare (79-acre) site near Wentworth that houses the county opportunity center for the handicapped, and the 97-hectare (240-acre) campus of Rockingham Community College at Wentworth, which has over 4.8 kilometers (3 miles) of nature trails. In 1975 A. G. Farris donated nearly 110 hectares (270 acres) of land to the town of Mayodan for development as a recreational park. Accessible there at the present time are ball fields, tennis courts, lakes, picnic shelters, and nature trails for public recreation.

The undulating terrain of Rockingham County was formed 150 million to 180 million years ago in the Triassic period at the beginning of the Mesozoic era. During its formative period the Dan River valley, one of only four Triassic basins in North Carolina, was inundated by a vast freshwater lake surrounded by extensive marshes. In the valley's subtropical climate flourished giant ferns, rushes, cycads (palm-like trees), and conifers. During the Mesozoic Age reptiles predominated, and dinosaurs, saurians, fishes, and bivalves inhabited the valley swamps.

The characteristic rock formations of the period are red, brown, yellow, and gray mudstones and clay stones; black shale; carbonaceous shale; sandstone; and conglomerates. In the late Triassic period massive earthquakes triggered severe faulting in the basin, and the lake bed strata were elevated as much as 50 degrees. Over millions of years the slippage may have been as much as 2,400 meters (8,000 feet), and the resulting jagged, mountainous ridges that border the basin eventually weathered into the rolling hills typical of the Piedmont.

Rich fossil remains of prehistoric flora and fauna can be found throughout the valley in the clays, shales, and coal veins. Petrified wood from the Triassic forest is abundant on the slopes of the basin; fossil ferns and a variety of leaves are common; and the rocks themselves exhibit mud cracks and ripple patterns from the ancient lake bed. In the carbonaceous shale the minute bivalve shells of the mollusks of the genera *Estheria* and *Posidonia* are plentiful. In 1856 state geologist Ebenezer Emmons discovered three vertebrae of a saurian, an ancestor of the alligator, which he named the Leaksville saurian.

The most significant recent fossil discoveries have come from the Solite quarry near Eden. The first dinosaur tracks ever found in North Carolina were discovered there in October, 1970. The creature to which the tracks were attributed, identified as a Yaleosaurus, was probably

3

about 3 meters (10 feet) tall and walked upright on a three-toed foot. A team from Yale University recently uncovered a number of fossils in the quarry, the most interesting of which was a well-preserved lizard skeleton that has been dubbed the Solite lizard.

The Triassic rocks have produced not only good soil in the bottomlands but mineral resources for the county as well. Through the years quarries have been opened for the production of crushed stone and gravel. The river itself is dredged for sand, but more important are the clays and shales, which have helped make North Carolina a leading producer of bricks and clay products.

Denison Olmsted, professor of chemistry at the University of North Carolina, first called attention to the presence of coal in the region in a geological report made in 1824, and the Dan River coalfield received a thorough examination by Ebenezer Emmons during the 1850s. The coal vein is narrow and sparse and in some places only a few centimeters wide, but during the Civil War coal was mined extensively on the Wade plantation, just upstream from Leaksville, where several dozen coal pits are still visible. The coal was shipped downriver by bateaux to Danville, Virginia, then the railhead of the Richmond & Danville Railroad. By the end of the nineteenth century, geologists had concluded that the Dan River coalfield was too deficient in coal deposits to be of commercial value.

Two other minerals—iron ore and mica—have been mined in the county. The iron ore present in the Haw River basin occurs on the end of a belt of titaniferous magnetite ore that extends across Guilford County. An ironworks was established on Big Troublesome Creek as early as 1770 and may have been operated until the end of the eighteenth century. The mine, located in the Midway community, was reopened in 1869 for two years as the Dannemora Mine. It was leased by Thomas Graham of Philadelphia, who had earlier established the North Carolina Center Iron Company. In 1880 two deep shafts were dug into the deposit and equipped with an incline. A steam engine was used to pump water from the mine, which was operated by English and local miners. The ore was hauled by wagon and rail to the company's Tuscarora Forge near Friendship in Guilford County.

Mica exists in commercial quantities in the Price community. Mica mining began sometime prior to 1890 at the Long Tom Smith mine owned by Randolph Smith, continued intermittently during the ensuing decades, and peaked between 1942 and 1945. Over a dozen mines have been operated in the Price area, the largest in recent years being the Knight mine, which opened in 1943 and included a number of production shafts.

The leading natural resource of the county is water, which is valued as a source of power. Waterpower was first harnessed by the early pioneers for gristmills, which began to appear during the eighteenth century within a few years after initial settlement. During the nineteenth cen-

A contemporary view of the Dan River, Rockingham County's most important waterway. Photograph (1981) supplied by the author.

tury both the Smith and the Mayo rivers were utilized to generate waterpower, steam power, and hydroelectric power for use by textile mills. In the twentieth century Duke Power Company has erected large steam-generation plants on the Dan River and Belews Creek. The Dan River Steam Station at Eden began operations in 1949 and is capable of producing 375,000 kilowatts of electricity. The Belews Creek Steam Station, opened in 1974 and equipped with the largest coal-fired units in the Duke Power system, is capable of producing 2,286,000 kilowatts of electricity. The water at both stations is used for cooling. In 1976 a distinctly water-related industry, Miller Brewing Company of Milwaukee, announced that it would build a brewery in Eden. The facility began operations in 1978 and is the largest single industrial plant ever to locate in the county.

Native People

Prehistoric people left no written records, but much information about their lives can be gleaned from their artifacts of stone, clay, and bone. Although there has been no systematic archaeological investigation of the county, archaeologist Joffre L. Coe and his staff from the University of North Carolina at Chapel Hill and various local amateur archaeologists have conducted excavations in the Dan valley. Precisely when man began to enter the Dan and Haw river valleys may never be ascertained, but collectors have found a few projectile points that are 8,000 to 10,000 years old. In the formative period of the piedmont cultures, according to Professor Coe, people wandered in small groups and hunted big game. Their campsites, where they probably were sheltered by rude brush windbreaks, are usually found on low ridges near small streams. Most common in Rockingham County are the chipped stone points, axes, scrapers, and celts of the Guilford culture, dating

5

from about 4000 to 3000 B.C. To a later culture, the Savannah River, are attributed soapstone vessels and polished stone implements unearthed in the county.

Beginning about 500 A.D. the piedmont Indians began to make pottery. These people lived in circular wigwams made of bark and surrounded by a palisade or log stockade. They fished, gathered freshwater mussels and snails, hunted deer and elk, and grew corn, squash, and beans. Their artifacts include a variety of stone projectile points and tools, a wide array of bone implements, several types of clay pots and bowls, tobacco pipes made of stone or clay, gaming pieces, bone and shell beads, and a shell death mask.

By the time European discovery and exploration of America began in the sixteenth and seventeenth centuries, two dozen Indian tribes that spoke dialects of the Siouan language dwelt in the Piedmont. Within two centuries after the Europeans first entered their realm, these tribes had vanished as a result of warfare and disease.

The Dan River valley was inhabited by only one known tribe, identified variously as the Saura, Sara, or Cheraw, which arrived about 1674 and departed by 1710. The Saura first encountered Europeans in 1540 when a Spanish expedition led by Hernando DeSoto arrived at the tribal village of Xualla in the Blue Ridge Mountains. The Saura later moved to the Trading Ford on the Yadkin River, where John Lederer, traveling out of Virginia, visited them in 1670. Following the murder of a Virginia trader on the Yadkin in 1673, the Saura moved to the Dan River valley and there established two village complexes: Upper Sauratown, near Walnut Cove in present-day Stokes County, and Lower Sauratown, near Eden. They were preyed upon by northern Seneca and by 1711 were living with the Keyauwee in upper South Carolina near the present-day town of Cheraw.

The Cheraw tribe fought against the Tuscarora in the Tuscarora War of 1712 and against the Seneca in the Yamassee War of 1715. Although the tribe had at one time numbered more than a thousand, by the mid-eighteenth century the population had dwindled to fewer than a hundred. Some of the remaining Saura joined the remnant of the Catawba tribe, and others may have gone back into North Carolina, where they became ancestors of the modern Lumbee.

Professor Coe examined the Lower Sauratown site in 1938, and during the 1970s archaeologists at the University of North Carolina at Chapel Hill conducted a series of excavations at Upper Sauratown. These excavations revealed that the Saura villages had been stockaded and that the inhabitants had lived in round lodges made of bark. The Indians tended fields of corn, beans, and squash as well as peach orchards. Bone fishhooks, stone fish dams, and mussel shells attest to the Saura's dependence upon the Dan River. The tribe's trash pits contain bones of deer, elk, bear, and small game. Archaeological evidence suggests that the wide variety of stone and bone tools and weapons were being supplanted by European traders' guns, steel knives, hatchets, and hoes. The intricate clay-and-bone beads and quillwork were replaced by copper bells and glass beads supplied by the traders. The Madison cemetery site, excavated by amateur archaeologists, has yielded a wealth of trade goods, including over 25,000 glass beads.

Although the Indians had departed before the first English explorers entered the Dan valley, their fields left a mark on the land. After visiting the site of the former Saura settlement in 1733, William Byrd II (1674-1744), Virginia planter and colonial official, wrote:

It must have been a great misfortune to them [the Indians] to be obliged to abandon so beautiful a dwelling, where the air is wholesome, and the soil equal in fertility to any in the world. The [Dan] river is about eighty yards wide, always confined within its lofty banks, and rolling down its waters, as sweet as milk, and as clear as crystal. There runs a charming level, of more than a mile square, that will bring forth like the lands of Egypt, without being overflowed once a year. There is scarce a shrub in view to intercept your prospect, but grass as high as a man on horseback.

Scattered throughout remote areas in North Carolina and adjacent states, small groups of Indian people survived by intermingling with white people and adopting their culture. Although these bands of mixed-breed Indians, often called Melungeons, lived mainly in the eastern part of the state, the hills in northwestern Rockingham County have long harbored such a community. This settlement, known as Goinstown, came into existence before the Civil War and at one time numbered several hundred inhabitants. By 1930, 150 Indians comprising 25 families, most of them small farmers or tenants, resided in the area. The county provided the Indians with a separate public school that served the community until the county's schools were consolidated into a single system during the 1950s. The author of a study conducted in 1936 concluded that with no stable institutions the people of Goinstown would gradually depart; however, a small number of these Indians remain in the county at the present time.

II. THE COLONIAL AND REVOLUTIONARY PERIOD

Discovery

The impending sale of the Carolinas by the Lords Proprietors to the British crown resulted in the appointment in 1728 of a commission to survey and adjust the long-disputed boundary between the colonies of Virginia and North Carolina. This commission was to consist of four representatives from North Carolina and three from Virginia. William Byrd II was selected as one of the three Virginia commissioners, and William Mayo and Alexander Irvine were the Virginia surveyors. Beginning at the Outer Banks in the spring of 1728 and moving westward, the survey party reached the Dan River by October. Indians who accompanied the party as hunters found plentiful game in the Dan River valley—mostly deer, bear, and wild turkey.

Byrd, an avid student of the Bible, named the Dan River for one of the lost tribes of Israel. He was captivated by the waterway, declaring that it "seem'd the most beautiful River that I ever saw." Byrd was also awed by the appearance of the land in the river valley. In his *History of the Dividing Line betwixt Virginia and North Carolina* he wrote:

> All the Land we Travell'd over . . . from the river Irvin [Smith] to Sable Creek [Wolf Island], is exceedingly rich. . . . Besides whole Forests of Canes, that adorn the Banks of the River and Creeks thereabouts, the fertility of the Soil throws out such a Quantity of Winter Grass, that Horses and Cattle might keep themselves in Heart all the cold Season without the help of any Fodder.

For their services the North Carolina commissioners received a grant of land in the Dan River valley. William Byrd subsequently acquired 20,000 acres of the land embracing this grant and named it the Land of Eden. Attempting to promote settlement in his Eden, Byrd touted the healthy elevation and air, the fertility of the soil, and the perfection of the climate; he even claimed that the valley could support vineyards and the production of silk, hemp, flax, cotton, fruit trees, and rice.

In 1733 Byrd returned with his friend William Mayo to survey his tract. He camped in the area in September and October, completed the survey, and visited the former site of Lower Sauratown, which he later purchased as part of a tract of 6,000 acres. Byrd reluctantly left his Eden, declaring, "Happy will be the people destined for so wholesome a situation, where they may live to fulness of days, and which is much better still, with much content and gayety of heart."

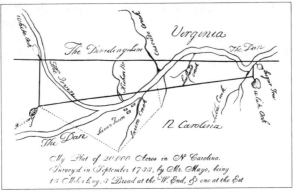

Shown on this plat map is the tract of 20,000 acres of Dan River bottomland acquired by William Byrd II in 1733. Byrd dubbed this tract the Land of Eden because of the lush quality of the vegetation found there. Byrd inserted this map in the manuscript of his *A Journey to the Land of Eden in the Year 1733*. The map is here reproduced from William K. Boyd, *William Byrd's Histories of the Dividing Line betwixt Virginia and North Carolina* (Raleigh: North Carolina Historical Commission, 1929), facing p. 268.

Early Settlement

William Byrd's prophecy of a prosperous settlement in his Eden was not immediately fulfilled, although by the mid-eighteenth century the North Carolina backcountry experienced a period of phenomenal growth. Thousands of settlers from Pennsylvania, New Jersey, Maryland, and Virginia entered the region by way of the Great Wagon Road, which extended from Philadelphia southwestward through the Shenandoah valley into the Carolinas. South of Big Lick (modern Roanoke) the road forked into several branches, one of which entered present-day Rockingham County in the upper Mayo valley. These backcountry pioneers were for the most part English, Scotch-Irish, and German, but the Rockingham County frontier was populated almost entirely by the Scotch-Irish. Backcountry settlement tripled and quadrupled during the two ensuing decades, and by the time of the American Revolution nearly half the population of the province of North Carolina resided in the interior.

Available evidence suggests that the earliest settlement in Rockingham County occurred in the Troublesome Creek valley. Several years ago a fallen gravestone was discovered in the Speedwell Presbyterian Cemetery; the stone bore this inscription: "Milton Bennett, Infant of Geo. Benet, died June 17th, 1739." This is the oldest known grave marker in the county. No other information about this family has been found, but the marked gravestone and cemetery suggest that a settlement of some sort existed in that vicinity at that early date.

9

When the crown purchased the Carolina grant in 1729, one of the Lords Proprietors, John Lord Carteret, Earl Granville, declined to sell his share, and by 1744 the northern half of North Carolina became known as the Granville District. The earl's agents issued land grants to those who settled in the district but in general mismanaged it, creating dissatisfaction and unrest among the settlers. By 1750 the provincial attorney general, Robert Jones, and Daniel Weldon were surveying the Dan valley and selling the land. Among the earliest grants of land in present-day Rockingham County were those to John Jude on the Mayo River in 1752, to William Rice and Owen Sullivant on Matrimony Creek in 1753, to John Boyd on Troublesome Creek in 1755, and to Thomason Harris on Hogans Creek in 1755.

Colonial Life

The influx of new settlers created a need for county government. Rockingham County was formed in 1785 from the northern portion of Guilford County, which had been created in 1770 from portions of Orange and Rowan counties. North Carolina's colonial counties were governed by appointed justices of the peace, who made up the quarterly county court, and by a sheriff, who was aided by deputies and constables. Among the known inhabitants of the lower Dan River valley were James Watkins and James Hampton, who were appointed constables in June, 1753. Others who served the area of present-day Rockingham County as early road overseers, tax collectors, or jury

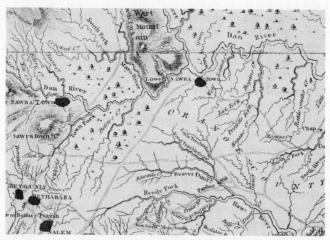

This portion of a map of North Carolina drawn by John Abraham Collet and published in 1770 delineates the approximate present location of Rockingham County. From original map held by William P. Cumming, Davidson; reproduced courtesy Division of Archives and History, Raleigh.

members were Valentine Allen, Joseph Scales, Joseph Cloud, Joseph Tate, Robert Ralston, John McMahon, John Lemon, and Charles Mitchel.

The oldest church in the county is the Speedwell Presbyterian congregation on Troublesome Creek, which is believed to have been organized by 1759. As early as 1755 Presbyterian missionary Hugh McAden held services in the region, and David Caldwell entered missionary work in 1764, becoming pastor of nearby Buffalo Church in present-day Guilford County. By 1768 the Speedwell congregation called Samuel Leak, a graduate of Princeton College, to be its pastor. Another Presbyterian congregation in the same area was Haw River Church, which existed until 1836. By 1793 James McGready was serving as pastor of both Speedwell and Haw River churches.

More numerous than the Presbyterians were the Baptists, who established several churches in the county during the eighteenth century. The county's earliest Baptist church records pertain to congregations located at Matrimony Creek, organized by 1776; Wolf Island (1777); and Lick Fork (1786). These churches are active Primitive Baptist congregations at the present time.

The only important colonial industry in the county was milling. By 1753 Aaron and Joseph Pinson had erected a mill at High Rock Ford on the Haw River. The mill is no longer extant, but portions of the rock milldam can still be found on the site. John Davis had established a mill on a branch of the Haw River by 1760. It was sold to William Patrick (1738-1771) in March, 1763, and the property is still owned by Patrick's descendants. The Patrick family was the source of several generations of millers in the county. Joseph Cloud, who settled on the Dan River in 1755, operated a mill on Rockhouse Creek by 1759. A mill on Matrimony Creek was mentioned in a road survey of July, 1764.

Joseph Buffington (1737-1796), a Quaker ironmaster from Chester County, Pennsylvania, established Speedwell Furnace, an ironworks on Troublesome Creek, in 1770. Buffington erected a furnace and bloomery but by 1772 had sold them and moved to South Carolina. With the outbreak of the American Revolution the production of iron was encouraged, but a committee appointed by the Provincial Congress in 1776 chose not to reopen the Speedwell Furnace. The facility's forge was probably used during the war to repair weapons inasmuch as both the British and American armies utilized the site as a campground.

Commerce in the region was handled chiefly by British and Scottish merchants who operated stores in Virginia and in the Cape Fear valley. Typical of these frontier merchants was Charles Gallaway (d. 1795), who in 1765 purchased land south of the Dan River overlooking a ford. There he established his plantation, known as Rose Hill, and his store, Gallaway and Company.

The first settlement in the county was at Lower Sauratown near a ford on the Dan River. The Byrd tracts, which consisted altogether of

26,000 acres, were sold in October, 1755, by William Byrd III to Francis and Simon Farley, merchants of Antigua, who were visiting in Virginia at the time. By 1769 James Parke Farley, a son of Francis, had been sent to manage the estate. After removing squatters, Farley established a plantation on which he installed livestock and a hundred slaves imported from Antigua. Farley brought his wife Elizabeth, the daughter of William Byrd III, and his four daughters to live on the Dan River; and in 1775 he erected a manor house, known as Belleview, in which he resided for the remainder of his life. Letters from Farley's wife to her father mention the plantation, tobacco crops, and the family's regular contacts by wagon with Virginia. The Farley letters are the earliest documentation of tobacco culture in the county, and it is possible that the Farleys were the first residents to grow the crop that later became the county's most important agricultural product.

Just prior to the Revolution a young English gentleman, John F. D. Smyth, while on an extensive tour through the colonies, passed through Lower Sauratown in the course of his journey from Hillsborough to Kentucky. After losing his way on a barely discernible forest path, Smyth arrived at the settlement, where he found lodging with a Bailey family who dwelt in a one-room cabin. Considering Smyth's status, it must be assumed that the Farleys were not at home at the time. Smyth remained in Lower Sauratown for ten days and became enamored of fifteen-year-old Betsy Bailey, "a most lovely charming brunette . . . of a shape and features perfectly exquisite and expressive, and endued with a mind and manners, mild, gentle, and delicate, yet quite in a state of nature. . . ." Possibly because of his apparent captivation with young Betsy, Smyth made little reference to the Farley plantation other than that it was "extremely valuable" and that it possessed "a vast body of excellent and most valuable land, containing thirty-three thousand acres, of which more than nine thousand are exceedingly rich low grounds. . . ." He did mention, however, that the trade of the settlement went either downriver or overland to Petersburg and Richmond, Virginia.

Despite news of Indian depredations on the upper Smith River, Smyth reluctantly decided to terminate his pleasant dalliance with Betsy, who, Smyth wrote, "absolutely gained on my affections every moment." The country north of the Dan River was virtually deserted as a result of Indian raids, but Smyth managed to reach a Virginia fort safely after being guided part of the way by a band of warring Indians.

The colonial settlers of present-day Rockingham County with few exceptions resided on farms of a few hundred acres, grew grains and tobacco, and tended herds of cattle, pigs, and sheep. Such an economy, based on subsistence farming, required few slaves; but eventually great plantations emerged on the rich soil of the Dan River valley.

Although no pre-Revolutionary dwellings are known to exist in the county, it is likely that most of the inhabitants resided in one- or two-room log houses with stone chimneys. Betsy Bailey's father, who owned a few slaves, was described by Smyth as a "common plain back wood's planter." There was only one room in the Bailey home, with one bed. Smyth noted that he and the Bailey children slept on a pallet on the floor, and he indicated that the slaves, young children, grown sons, and three grown daughters all slept in the same room.

The Revolutionary Era

The period from 1765 to 1775 was one of unrest, social upheaval, and violence in North Carolina. The Regulator protest movement began in 1765 and ended in defeat at the Battle of Alamance in 1771. The Regulators, who were backcountry men, had demanded reform of a corrupt, inefficient provincial government dominated by eastern planters and merchants. The movement was centered in Orange and Rowan counties, although Regulator petitions bearing the signatures of settlers of present-day Rockingham County are known to exist.

From 1771 to 1775 North Carolina was immersed in the mainstream of events leading to the American Revolution. After more than a century of neglect by British colonial authorities, the American colonies had matured politically; but during these years Parliament and British imperial officials initiated efforts to generate additional revenues from the colonies through new taxes and stricter enforcement of colonial trade laws. The colonial leadership chose to counter the new British policies through petitions, protest, economic boycott, and finally war. By 1775 the authority of the royal governor had deteriorated to such an extent that the province of North Carolina was being governed by county and town committees of safety and provincial congresses. Among the Guilford County delegates to the Third Provincial Congress of August, 1775, were Alexander Martin, Thomas Henderson, Nathaniel Williams, and James Parke Farley. At this Congress Charles Gallaway was appointed a member of the Salisbury District Committee of Safety.

The county's most prominent citizen of the eighteenth century, Alexander Martin (1738-1807), a native of New Jersey and a Princeton graduate, arrived in Salisbury about 1760. By December, 1761, he had established his plantation, known as Danbury, on the Dan River at the mouth of Jacob's Creek. (He later maintained an additional residence at Guilford Courthouse.) Martin was a merchant, planter, attorney, and county justice. He became active in the Revolutionary movement and was a delegate to the Second and Third provincial congresses. He was appointed lieutenant colonel of the Second North Carolina Continental Regiment and served in campaigns in South Carolina and at Moores Creek Bridge. After Martin was promoted to colonel, his regiment was sent to join George Washington's army in Pennsylvania, where it saw active service at Brandywine and Germantown. During the engagement at Germantown a thick fog obscured visibility on portions of the

Alexander Martin was Rockingham County's "most prominent citizen of the eighteenth century." Engraving from Hampton L. Carson (ed.), *History of the Celebration of the One Hundredth Anniversary of the Promulgation of the Constitution of the United States* (Philadelphia: J. B. Lippincott, 2 volumes, 1889), I, facing p. 230.

battlefield, resulting in confusion and panic among some of the American troops. Martin and other American officers were later court-martialed for cowardice in connection with this incident, but Martin was subsequently absolved of the charge; nevertheless, he resigned his commission in November, 1777, and returned to North Carolina. He represented Guilford County in the state Senate from 1778 to 1781 and during the latter year, while serving as Speaker of the Senate, became acting governor when Governor Thomas Burke was captured by loyalists. Martin was later elected governor in his own right and won reelection in 1783 and 1784. In December, 1786, he was elected by the General Assembly as a member of the Continental Congress and the following year was chosen as one of North Carolina's five delegates to the Constitutional Convention at Philadelphia.

The county's chief contribution to the war effort during the early years of the Revolution was through the activities of the local militia regiment commanded by James Martin (1742-1834), brother of Alexander Martin. James Martin had moved to the Haw River valley in 1774, and by the end of the war he resided in Stokes County. The militia was called into service for the Moores Creek Bridge campaign in February, 1776; for the Cherokee campaign in June, 1776; for the Battle of Guilford Courthouse in March, 1781; for the campaign against Wilmington in October, 1781; and for the apprehension of loyalist raiders on several occasions during the war.

The war did not come to northern Guilford County until 1781, when the American army commanded by General Nathanael Greene retreated into the region while being pursued by British forces under the command of Lord Cornwallis. No battles were fought in present-day Rockingham, but the area was an important staging area just prior to the Battle of Guilford Courthouse. The Americans established bases for rendezvous and supply at the Troublesome Creek Ironworks and at High Rock Ford.

At Guilford Courthouse in February, Greene divided his army into a main body and a screening detachment of light troops commanded by

Colonel Otho Williams. By feinting toward the fords of the upper Dan River, Williams drew Cornwallis away from Greene's main army, which safely crossed the Dan into Virginia on February 13. Cornwallis, having been duped, pushed Williams and the cavalry commanded by Colonel Henry Lee across present-day Rockingham and Caswell counties. The British cavalry, commanded by the notorious Colonel Banastre Tarleton, encamped at the Troublesome Creek Ironworks on the day Greene crossed the Dan.

Cornwallis then marched to Hillsborough, raised the royal standard, and proclaimed the province "liberated." By February 23 Greene recrossed the Dan and established bases at High Rock Ford, the ironworks, and Boyd's Mill on Reedy Fork Creek. The Guilford County militia under Colonel James Martin joined Greene at High Rock Ford. On March 12 the Americans marched leisurely toward Guilford

This pencil sketch of the Troublesome Creek Ironworks was rendered ca. 1900 by Henry Denny, an otherwise unidentified amateur artist. Sketch in the possession of J. Lee Pharr, Concord; reproduced from copy in North Carolina Collection, University of North Carolina Library, Chapel Hill.

Courthouse, where three days later they engaged the British in an indecisive battle. Greene retreated in the rain to the ironworks, where his army rested and stragglers were gathered. The camp was fortified, but Cornwallis had suffered crippling losses at Guilford Courthouse and retreated to Wilmington, the nearest British base.

During the postwar years several men in northern Guilford County provided local leadership. James Gallaway and John Leak represented the county in the state House of Commons in 1783, and the following year Gallaway was elected to the state Senate. James Hunter and Hugh Challis were county justices in 1782, and Hunter was sheriff in 1784-1785 and county treasurer from 1783 to 1785. William Bethell, John May, and John Hunter were deputy sheriffs under James Hunter. Alexander Martin and his brother-in-law Thomas Henderson, who was clerk of the county court, began development of the village of Martinville at the county seat. Alexander Martin continued his distinguished political career in the state Senate, as governor from 1789 to 1792, as a delegate to the federal Constitutional Convention of 1787, and as a United States senator from 1793 to 1799.

The area comprising present-day Rockingham County continued to be developed as a new wave of immigrants from Pennsylvania, Maryland, and Virginia—many of them Revolutionary War veterans—settled grants throughout the region. In 1782 John Cummins and Peter Perkins sought permission from the state legislature to erect a gristmill on Troublesome Creek, and Samuel Wardlow petitioned the body for the privilege of establishing a mill on Rockhouse Creek. James Wright opened a tavern at his home on the Haw River in 1783, and the following year John Dearing and Peter O'Neal erected mills on Belews Creek and Hogans Creek respectively.

After the war, efforts were made to reopen the Troublesome Creek Ironworks. In 1783 Colonel Archibald Lytle of Hillsborough, a veteran of service with the Sixth North Carolina Continental Regiment, formed a partnership with Peter and Constantine Perkins for the purpose of acquiring the ironworks property. Peter Perkins purchased Lytle's interest in 1786 and then sold the ironworks tract to George Hairston and John Marr of Henry County, Virginia. Hairston and Marr hired Dr. Benjamin Jones as manager, and by 1790 the forge and furnace at the ironworks were operating with the services of thirty-five slaves. During his southern tour President George Washington, who had spent the previous evening at the home of Alexander Martin in Martinville, paused at the ironworks on the morning of June 3, 1791, and took breakfast with the Jones family.

III. A NEW COUNTY

Birth of the County

The population of the North Carolina backcountry increased substantially after the close of the Revolutionary War, resulting in the creation of several new counties during the 1780s. On December 29, 1785, the General Assembly enacted legislation that created Rockingham County from approximately the northern half of Guilford County and appointed William Dent, John Hamilton, Charles Bruce, Samuel Henderson, Joshua Smith, and Abraham Philips as commissioners to survey and establish the new county's boundary line, which was to run east and west from "Haw river bridge, near James Martins. . . ."

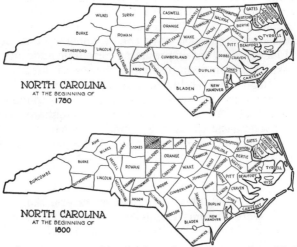

Rockingham County was created in 1785 from the northern portion of Guilford County. Maps by L. Polk Denmark; reproduced from David Leroy Corbitt, *The Formation of the North Carolina Counties, 1663-1943* (Raleigh: State Department of Archives and History, 1950), Appendix II.

The assembly chose to name the new county for Charles Watson-Wentworth, second Marquess of Rockingham (1730-1782). Rockingham was a leading Whig and was prime minister of Britain from 1765 to 1766 and again in 1782. His popularity in America was assured when he secured repeal of the hated Stamp Act in 1766 and led the ministry that initiated negotiations to terminate the Revolutionary War. From 1768 to 1781 he had been the leading Parliamentary opponent of both the government's American policy and the war.

Rockingham County was named for Charles Watson-Wentworth, second Marquess of Rockingham. Oil portrait (date unknown) attributed to studio of Joshua Reynolds; reproduced courtesy National Portrait Gallery, London, in *"The Dye Is Now Cast": The Road to American Independence, 1774-1776* (Washington: Smithsonian Institution Press for the National Portrait Gallery, 1975), Plate 107.

The first session of the new county's quarterly court was convened in February, 1786, at the plantation of Adam Tate near Eagle Falls on the south side of the Dan River. The justices of the peace of this first court, most of whom were veterans of the Revolutionary War, were James Hunter, Samuel Henderson, George Peay, Hugh Challis, Thomas Henderson, Adam Tate, James Gallaway, John Leak, Joshua Smith, Peter O'Neal, Abraham Philips, William Bethell, John May, and John Hunter. County justices were charged with the responsibility of hearing civil suits and minor criminal cases, providing for public buildings, probating decedents' estates, ruling on individual cases of lunacy, caring for orphans and illegitimate children, and maintaining public roads and bridges. Justices were appointed, generally from among the landed, slave-owning gentry. All the members of Rockingham County's first court were slaveholders: the average justice owned nine slaves.

The court established a commission to select a permanent site for the county seat, oversee construction of the public buildings, and levy a tax for two years to finance construction of two public buildings. The court also appointed a coroner, a ranger, militia officers, patrollers (for the control of slaves), constables, and road overseers. Some of the first county officers were Thomas Henderson, clerk of court; John Hunter, register of deeds; Abraham Philips, surveyor; and Nathaniel Williams, state attorney. William Bethell succeeded Henderson as clerk of court in 1792 and served until his death in 1804.

Prominent in the county's early development was Abraham Philips (1755-1836), who settled in present-day Rockingham by 1779 and eventually owned a 700-acre plantation on Rockhouse Creek and accumulated thirty-one slaves. As the county surveyor, Philips established the new county's southern boundary line and also surveyed the sites of Leaksville (1795) and Wentworth (1799), the county's earliest towns. In addition, he served as a county justice for forty years, keeper of the weights and measures, a trustee of the town of Wentworth, and chairman of the county court in 1807. A Jeffersonian Republican, he was elected to three terms in the state House of Commons and to nine terms in the state Senate. After having served as a militia captain during the

Revolutionary War, Philips became colonel of the county's militia regiment in 1810 and the following year was promoted to brigadier general, retaining that rank until his resignation in 1817. He is buried near his plantation house, a portion of which is standing at the present time. It is one of the county's oldest structures.

The county's first sheriff, John May, was ordered to bring to the next session of county court as a symbol of his office a white wand 8 feet long and an inch in diameter. Constables were authorized to carry 6-foot-long white wands with black tips. Law and order was maintained by the sheriff, who was assisted by constables in each district of the county. Shortly after the county was established, a jail, whipping post, and stocks were erected at the county seat. Among the early attorneys licensed to practice before the county court was Andrew Jackson (in November, 1787).

A Citizen's Responsibilities

Taxes were low during the early years of the nation's history, but the citizen had many obligations that are unknown to his modern counterpart, who pays considerable taxes and only occasionally serves on jury duty. The white male citizen of the eighteenth and nineteenth centuries paid taxes, served frequently on jury duty, maintained public roads and bridges from time to time, was frequently called upon to serve on various county commissions, performed periodic duty with the slave patrol, and was a member of the local militia. Each county maintained at least one militia regiment in which most able-bodied adult males were enrolled. The county was divided into captain's districts corresponding to militia companies. These districts served as geographical subdivisions for the collection of taxes. The county's first militia officers were Colonel Samuel Henderson, Lieutenant Colonel

This jury ticket certified that Thomas Gallaway served for five days as a juror in Rockingham County Superior Court in 1839 and authorized the county trustee to pay Gallaway $5.50 for his attendance and other expenses. From Rockingham County Miscellaneous Records, L-Z, 1793-1925, folder marked "Jury Tickets, 1839," Archives, Division of Archives and History, Raleigh.

James Hunter, Majors John May and Peter O'Neal, and Captains William Bethell, John Leak, Abraham Philips, George Peay, and James Gallaway. All of these men had participated in the Revolutionary War.

Early Political Leadership

From among the landed gentry came the area's leadership at the state level. James Gallaway, the county's first state senator, compiled an impressive record, serving on numerous legislative committees and sponsoring legislation. Gallaway was active in promoting navigation of the Roanoke and Dan rivers and introduced the bill that resulted in establishment of the Dismal Swamp Canal Company, which was chartered in 1790. The county's first representatives in the state House of Commons were William Bethell and Peter Perkins. Thomas Henderson was elected to the Council of State in 1795.

In this early period the county was strongly Jeffersonian Antifederalist in politics. In the state Senate James Gallaway attempted unsuccessfully to block the call for a state convention to ratify the federal constitution. However, when the convention opened in Hillsborough in July, 1788, Rockingham County was represented by Gallaway, William Bethell, Abraham Philips, John May, and Charles Gallaway—all of whom were Antifederalists opposed to ratification. Gallaway was second only to Willie Jones of Halifax in exercising leadership of the Antifederalists at the convention, and the ratification effort failed.

At a second convention, held at Fayetteville in November, 1789, Federalist delegates dominated, and ratification of the Constitution was secured. Gallaway, the leading Antifederalist spokesman, nevertheless led a gallant but unsuccessful fight to delay the decision. He was successful, however, in securing passage of five amendments to be proposed to the United States Congress. The county was represented at the Fayetteville convention by Gallaway, Bethell, Philips, Isaac Clarke, and John Dabney, all of whom voted in the minority against ratification.

The First Courthouse

The county justices apparently intended to erect a courthouse near Eagle Falls, but the proposed location was challenged because it was not close enough to the geographic center of the county. Consequently, the county surveyor was requested to ascertain the approximate midpoint of the county, and on January 1, 1787, the General Assembly established a new commission and empowered it to locate the county seat "on the lands of Charles Mitchell on the east side of Big Rock House creek. . . ."

Ever alert to possible pecuniary gain, Constantine Perkins and Charles Gallaway in April, 1787, purchased from Mitchell a 200-acre tract located on Bear Swamp and Rocky branches. The commissioners ultimately selected a portion of this tract, a high ridge just east of Rockhouse Creek, as the site for the new county seat. On August 28, 1787, Perkins and Gallaway conveyed to the county one acre for public use, and during the August session the county court authorized the new courthouse to be occupied during the ensuing court session. The November term of the county court convened in the courthouse, which was then nearly complete, but not until the May, 1788, term was the builder, Richard Sharp, paid and the public buildings formally received by the justices. The present courthouse is located on or near the site of the original facility, and there is no evidence that the county seat was ever located at any place other than the Adam Tate house near Eagle Falls, where it existed from February, 1786, to August, 1787.

A detailed description of the county's first courthouse was recorded in the minutes of the November, 1792, session of the Guilford County Court. The Guilford justices were apparently considering work on their own courthouse and sent a committee to examine the neighboring county's facility. The committee reported that the Rockingham County courthouse was 36½ feet long, just over 24 feet wide, and a little over 11 feet to the "cornish." The porches were just over 9 feet long and 6 feet wide. The structure was weatherboarded with poplar "in an Ordinary manner." The interior courtroom was ceiled with pine 10 inches wide, and the floor was made of 6-inch pine. The benches were of pine, and the court's bench and bar were described as being "Elegantly Moulded and beaded . . . the Corner parts of the bench boxed & Caped in a Genteel manner." The building was underpinned with brick and covered with a chestnut-shingle roof. The courtroom was warmed by two fireplaces with one chimney. Alexander Sneed, a county justice, register of deeds, and former representative in the state House of Commons, responded in 1810 to a request from a Raleigh newspaper for information about Rockingham County by preparing a detailed sketch that was published in the paper and is now regarded as an important and valuable historical source. Sneed's 1810 sketch described the courthouse as "a tollerable wooden Court House, painted. . . ."

Life and Society in the New County

During this early period the county justices dealt with a wide range of social problems. Orphans and illegitimate children were bound to responsible citizens—girls to the age of eighteen and boys to the age of twenty-one. Boys were taught such crafts or trades as blacksmithing, shoemaking, coopering, or carpentry, in addition to learning to read, write, and do arithmetic. Overseers of the poor were first elected in February, 1790.

County justices dispensed punishment for offenses such as petty larceny, and both men and women were sentenced to time in the stocks and public whippings on the bare back. (The harshest sentence dispensed in

1788 was thirty-nine lashes.) One Sherwood Brock approached the court in February, 1787, with a request that it be recorded that his "left Ear [was] bit of [off] . . . in an affray with Robert Sanders." This request apparently stemmed from the fact that prior to the Revolution criminals had their ears nailed to stocks and then cropped upon release; thus a person with a missing ear might be identified as a former criminal, and Brock desired to be disassociated from that stigma.

The county court was responsible for the construction and maintenance of public roads, bridges, and ferries and for the licensing and regulation of gristmills and taverns. In November, 1787, Robert Gallaway was given permission to open a tavern at the county seat. The tavern rates established by the justices in August, 1787, were:

Good West India rum [per gallon]	£0.16.0
Taffie [per gallon]	10.8
Good Apple or Peach Brandy [per gallon]	10.8
Good Whiskey pr. [gallon]	10.8
Good Cyder pr. quart	.6
Strong Bear made of malt pr. qt.	.6
Warm Dinner	2.8
Breakfast or Supper	1.8
Lodging with clean Sheets pr. night	.8
Corn pr. Gallon	1.4
Oats pr. Gallon	1.0
Pasturage pr. night	.6
Stabledge pr. night	.6
Good Wine pr. Gallon	16.0
Corn Blades pr. Bundle	.1½

The county court, continuing the colonial tradition of offering bounties for the scalps of "vermin" such as panthers, wolves, wildcats, and even Indians, offered premiums of £1 for wolf scalps and 5 shillings for wildcats during the late 1780s.

The Founding of Wentworth

Although the county seat, known during the late 1780s and early 1790s as Rockingham Courthouse, consisted only of public buildings, a few houses, and a tavern, its central location and degree of business activity led to the establishment there on November 11, 1794, of the county's first post office. In order to accommodate the county court, the General Assembly in 1796 established a commission and authorized it to purchase up to forty acres of land from Robert Gallaway for the purpose of establishing a town to be named Wentworth. The act stipulated that if the land were not available from Gallaway the commissioners could move the county seat to a different location, but this provision so disturbed the county's citizens that the act was repealed. In 1798 the General Assembly responded by enacting a law that established the town of Wentworth at the existing county seat on the land of Robert Gallaway. Gallaway on February 16, 1799, generously sold (for 15 shillings) 125 acres of land to the trustees of the town of Wentworth. Shortly afterward, the trustees authorized the survey and sale of twenty-one town lots. No structure from this beginning period in the town's history is extant; however, in 1969 an archaeological excavation near Wentworth's Wright Tavern produced the remains of a one-and-one-half-story saltbox structure that probably stood during the town's formative period. Robert Williams had owned this house, as well as a plantation on the Dan River. Williams, a native of Virginia, was an attorney, a state senator from 1792 to 1795, and a United States congressman from 1797 to 1803. A Republican and supporter of President Thomas Jefferson, he served as territorial governor of Mississippi from 1805 to 1809.

The Founding of Leaksville

Leaksville was the dream of John Leak, who settled north of the Dan River on Matrimony Creek by 1773. Leak later added to his landholdings and by 1795 had selected as the site for a new town a high bluff near the confluence of the Dan and Smith rivers; Leak named the town Leaksville. Half-acre lots were laid off along the town's original streets: Water, Patrick, Henry, Hamilton, Washington, and Jay. Thomas Searcy made the first recorded purchase of a town lot in 1795. In anticipation of a tobacco trade, John Leak and Robert Coleman were appointed tobacco inspectors in 1796. The following year the General Assembly chartered the town with Leak, Sneed, Coleman, Nathaniel Seals, and Terry Hughes as the first commissioners. In 1800 the assembly approved the establishment of two taverns in the town.

According to Alexander Sneed's 1810 description, the town was "a most delightful Spot, and the best situated for trade, perhaps, of any in the County, as it commands a very extensive back Country, the produce of which (in consequence of a navigation free of obstructions up and down the [Dan] River) would inevitably center here." Natural obstructions to navigation of the Dan River, to which Sneed referred in 1810, were not removed until a decade later; consequently, the village did not grow very rapidly. By 1800 John Leak had lost much of his property through poor management.

Life in the Early Nineteenth Century

The population of Rockingham County grew slowly but steadily from 6,219 (including 1,105 slaves) in 1790 to 10,316 (including 2,114 slaves) in 1810. Then a backcountry outpost somewhat isolated from the rest of the state, Rockingham was populated mainly by small farmers who owned their own land, which, according to Alexander Sneed, endowed them with "an air of Independence, rarely to be met with in Countries where the labouring part of the community are Vassals and dependants on the Rich." Although a plantation aristocracy was beginning to develop in the Dan River valley, only about one quarter of the families in the county owned slaves in 1790. Nearly two thirds of the slaveholders owned five slaves or fewer, and only seven slaveholders had more than twenty.

In 1807 Sterling Ruffin of Brunswick County, Virginia, purchased a 1,000-acre Dan River plantation, and his letters to his son Thomas Ruffin indicate that he grew both corn and wheat extensively. The county's leading products, according to Alexander Sneed, were tobacco, cotton, beef, pork, flour, flaxseed, wheat, beeswax, and hemp. With the exception of wheat and flaxseed, which were exchanged for salt in Fayetteville, these commodities were marketed in Petersburg and Richmond. The county was blessed with abundant orchards, predominantly apple and peach, which produced "Vast quantities" of brandy and cider. There were 126 stills in the county in 1810 that together produced 30,900 gallons of whiskey and brandy valued at $15,400, which was almost half the total value of all products manufactured in the county. In 1810 Alexander Sneed cited the Dan River bottomlands, which he characterized as "mostly of a dark Rich mould, mixt with sand, and . . . well adapted to the culture of Indian corn . . . ," as "the most Valuable of any in the county." This land then sold for about $10.00 per acre.

Cotton gins and tanyards were common in the county during this period. The textile industry, which was home based, produced cotton, linen, and wool. In 1810 the county had 420 looms capable of weaving 85,000 yards of cloth valued at $16,500. Other manufactured products mentioned by Sneed were saddles, hats, boots, shoes, furniture, and rifles—the latter made by Captain Joshua Farrington and judged by Sneed to have been "equal, if not Superior to any imported. . . ." Mills were numerous, but Sneed enumerated only three in his 1810 report: James Patrick's mills on a branch of the Haw River and at the site of the Troublesome Creek Ironworks and Peter Bysor's mill at High Rock Ford on the Haw River. Flour "of the first quallity" was marketed in both Petersburg and Fayetteville. Other manufactured products were consumed at home and marketed outside of the county.

Sneed noted that his fellow citizens were "in general hospitable to Strangers, and appear to affect what may be called a Snug, rather than a Splendid way of living." Most of the houses inhabited by the county's residents in 1810 were constructed of logs, although a few frame dwellings then existed. High Rock on the Haw River and Willow Oaks on the Dan, two surviving examples of Federal architecture, are notable exceptions to this pattern. Joseph McCain, Jr., built High Rock, a three-story brick mansion, for his new bride, Polly Scales, before 1807. William Edward Brodnax of Brunswick County, Virginia, acquired the Willow Oaks property in 1811 from the Farley estate and conveyed it in 1820 to

Four surviving examples of Federal architecture in Rockingham County are High Rock (upper left), Willow Oaks (upper right), the Boxwoods (lower left), and the William Fewel house (lower right). Photographs at top from Lindley S. Butler, *Our Proud Heritage: A Pictorial History of Rockingham County, N.C.* (Bassett, Va.: Bassett Printing Corporation, 1971), p. 45. At lower left by Robert M. Leary & Associates, Ltd., Raleigh; reproduced in Diane Lea and Claudia Roberts, *An Architectural and Historical Survey of Madison, North Carolina* (Raleigh: North Carolina Department of Cultural Resources, Division of Archives and History, 1979), p. 10. At lower right courtesy Robert W. Carter, Jr., Reidsville.

his son Robert, who had constructed the elegantly trimmed frame house on the premises in 1818. Two other important examples of Federal architecture in Rockingham County are the Boxwoods, constructed of brick by Randal Duke Scales in Madison prior to 1810, and the nearby William Fewel house, a frame structure erected in 1815.

Alexander Sneed was optimistic about the future of culture and civilization in his county. There were no public schools in the county in 1810, but some of the gentry had received classical education at David Caldwell's academy in Guilford County. The professions were represented by law and medicine. Leading attorneys in this period were Theophilus Lacy, Thomas Settle, James T. Morehead, John May, and Rice Garland. Resident physicians in 1823 were Edward T. Brodnax, George W. Jones, and John Murry. The county's first graduate of the University of North Carolina was John Motley Morehead, who was a member of the class of 1817.

A wealthy bachelor such as Alexander Martin was able to live an elegant life. Martin frequented the nearby town of Salem, where he enjoyed the hospitality of the tavern. Mentioned in Martin's will were his coach, silver, china, a large library, a violin, a surveyor's instrument, silver candlesticks, a gold buckle, a gold-headed cane, silver spurs, and silver tumblers. Slaves freed by Martin's will were devised land grants.

In the nineteenth century, mineral springs were regarded as fashionable resorts, and the county boasted a well-known resort at Rockingham Springs or Lenox Castle. Residents of Salem and neighboring Moravian communities recorded their visits to the springs, and in 1790 Alexander Martin, then governor, convened a meeting of the Council of State there. By 1800 John Lenox was operating the springs, which was equipped with a patented shower; Lenox soon advertised his establishment as "The Castle of Thundertontrenck." At nearby High Rock, gentlemen could engage in horse racing, cockfighting, and card playing.

ROCKINGHAM MINERAL SPRINGS,

(Frequently called Lenox Castle.)

SITUATED in Rockingham County, North Carolina, directly on Messrs. Peck, Wellford & Co's, Stage Line, from Washington City to Milledgeville, Geo.; a high, handsome, healthy, and pleasant situation; the water (analyzed by Professor Olmstead,) impregnated with Sulphur, Carbon of Iron, and Magnesia, a solution of excellent MINERAL water; operating as a Cathartic, Diuretic, &c., strengthening and organizing the powers of digestion, Stomach, Bowels, Liver, Kidneys, &c., excellent in Liver affections, Dyspepsia, Debility, Eruptions, &c; invigorating the whole system. It is confidently believed that medical intelligence, if consulted, would recommend this water. The bathing establishment will be in good order.

The Proprietor is thankful, and under obligations to those that have patronized him, and informs visiters to the Springs, stage passengers, travellers, &c., that he will furnish good accommodations, during the approaching summer season; and he flatters himself that he has given general satisfaction to his friends and acquaintances heretofore.

JNO. J. WRIGHT.

June 1, 1837.   47-4t.

Advertisement for Rockingham Mineral Springs from *Fayetteville Observer*, July 12, 1837.

Archibald D. Murphey, a noted Hillsborough attorney, visited Rockingham Springs because of his poor health and ultimately purchased the property in 1807. Thomas Ruffin, later chief justice of the state supreme court and a relative of Murphey by marriage, also owned the springs for a time.

According to Alexander Sneed, dancing and horse racing were common amusements during this period. Sneed also alluded to "that vile and abominable practice of card playing &c which is so prevalent at our County Court Houses, Taverns &c and many other nefarious practices to delude the young and unwarry. . . ." Social activities tended to revolve about the taverns, especially at the county seat during court week. Wright Tavern in Wentworth, built in 1816 by William Wright, evolved into a rambling two-story frame dog-trot structure with numerous annexes and outbuildings. It was operated for many years by James Wright and then by his daughter Nannie Wright. By the twentieth cen-

Wright Tavern, erected at Wentworth by William Wright in 1816, was an important center of social activity during the antebellum era. Photograph courtesy Rockingham County Historical Society, Wentworth.

tury the tavern was called the Reid Hotel and was under the proprietorship of Numa R. Reid, who was also postmaster of the village. The tavern was the scene of informal discussions of court cases inasmuch as judges and attorneys boarded there during court sessions.

Alexander Sneed, ever the promoter of Leaksville, described Wentworth as "remarkable for nothing, except its high and healthy Situation it stands about three miles South of the River Dan, in a poor and broken part of the county, and near its Center. . . ." The little village was dominated by the courthouse, stone jail, stocks, and whipping post, and to this day exists primarily as the governmental center of the county.

Court minutes reveal that criminals, both men and women, were subject to punishment by whipping as late as the mid-nineteenth century. Public execution of a person convicted of a capital crime was a recognized social event. William Welsh, a convicted horse thief, was scheduled to be hanged at Wentworth in November, 1815. At the rear of Wright Tavern nearly a thousand people gathered to hear two hours of preaching and prayers before it was announced that the governor had pardoned Welsh. The convicted man's attorney, Archibald D. Murphey, had obtained the pardon by basing his plea solely on the ground that Welsh had been confined "in the most loathsome Prison in the State, and during [a] great Part of the Time of his Imprisonment, he has been in Irons."

Growth of religious institutions in the early nineteenth century was led by the Baptists, although both the Presbyterians and the Methodists were active in the county. The Sardis Baptist congregation was established by 1801, and the county's Baptist churches were organized in 1806 into the Country Line Association. At this early date Presbyterians were still concentrated in the Haw River valley in the three congregations of Speedwell, Haw River, and High Rock. Methodist circuit riders, including the noted Bishop Francis Asbury, began traveling into the county in the late eighteenth century, and early camp meetings were held near the present sites of Lowe's and Mount Carmel churches. The early Methodist churches in the county were Lowe's, organized by 1796; Salem, founded in 1799; Mount Carmel, established by 1805; and Bethlehem, founded several years later. The county's largest religious gathering during this period occurred at Wentworth in 1804 when the famed evangelist Lorenzo Dow preached to 1,500 people "in the freezing air and falling snow more than two hours."

In the early nineteenth century the Jeffersonian Republican party was dominant on both the national and state levels; however, bitter interparty battles and even factional intraparty squabbles occurred. A letter written by James Campbell to Thomas Ruffin in July, 1809, provides some insight into the nature of local political contests. Campbell, a recently naturalized American citizen, was a deputy clerk of court and an ally of local politicians James Gallaway, John Menzies, Nathaniel Scales, and Mark Harden. Alexander Sneed, a political enemy of these men, published a circular that derided high taxes and the mismanagement of the fiscal accounts of Gallaway, Menzies, and Scales with the intention of embarrassing them and causing the defeat of Scales and Harden in an impending election. Campbell characterized Sneed as a "Knave" who circulated "scurrilous assertions and clamorous sayings . . . a man of no principle no honour . . . a designing demagogue and will stick at nothing in furtherance of his nefarious schemes." Nothing is known of the outcome of this squabble except that Scales and Harden managed to win the contested election.

The War of 1812

The War of 1812 did not directly affect Rockingham County, but the county militia provided three companies of troops for possible participation in the conflict. Attached to the Sixth Regiment in 1812 was an infantry company of 53 men commanded by Captain William Lemon and a grenadier company of 79 men headed by Captain James Campbell of Wentworth; however, neither company saw active service. In November, 1814, when the British invasion of the Chesapeake Bay threatened the region, the state militia was again called up. A company of 115 men from Rockingham County, commanded by Captain George W. Barker, was mustered into the Fifth Regiment of detached state militia at Hillsborough. James Campbell was the regimental major.

Campbell's brief military tour is recorded in a letter to Thomas Ruffin. In January, 1815, Campbell wrote that his regiment was settled at "Camp Defiance," nearly a mile north of Norfolk, and had suffered since the previous December only eight deaths from illness—measles being the greatest offender. He reported, however, that 276 men were "sick and unfit for duty. . . ." Campbell's chief amusement was playing backgammon "for the first kisses of the ladies about Hillsboro. . . ." Unknown to him at this time was the fact that the war had been terminated two weeks earlier by the Treaty of Ghent, signed in Europe. The regiment soon returned home without seeing action against the British.

IV. ANTEBELLUM DEVELOPMENT

The Navigation Boom

By the end of the War of 1812 North Carolina began taking tentative steps toward awakening from the "Rip Van Winkle" years. The vision of state Senator Archibald D. Murphey of Hillsborough, who trained a generation of the state's leaders in his law office, provided the plan for future development of the state. In a series of comprehensive and influential reports presented to the state Senate between 1815 and 1818, Murphey, then chairman of the Senate Committee on Internal Improvements, recommended state expenditures for improved inland navigation and harbors. The legislatures of Virginia and North Carolina in 1815 rechartered the Roanoke Navigation Company (originally chartered in 1812), creating the impetus for economic development in the Roanoke valley.

In 1823, after several years of work, the rapids of the Roanoke River near Weldon were surmounted by a 9-mile canal that opened the upper Roanoke and its tributaries, the Dan and Staunton, to bateau navigation. With the construction of an extensive system of wing dams, sluices, short canals, and locks, the numerous shoals and rapids in the river were tamed. The Dan River was open to Leaksville by 1826, and two years later the new town of Madison was reached. Eventually the river was navigable as far upriver as Stokes County.

Bateaux were double-ended, shallow-draft, flat-bottomed craft manned by boatmen who used long poles to push against the river bottoms, thus propelling the vessel over water. Most boatmen of the antebellum era were slaves; after the Civil War most of them were free blacks. Steering was accomplished through the use of one or more long "sweeps" in the bow and stern of the vessel. The boats varied in length up to 60 feet and in width up to 8 feet. In transporting bulk cargoes—usually tobacco, flour, timber products, cotton, or grains—a bateau could carry up to six tons of freight. The Barnett family, developers of Leaksville, operated a bateau line and hired crewmen at $50.00 per season during the 1820s.

The Virginia towns through which the James River flowed—Richmond, Petersburg, and Norfolk—continued to dominate as markets for the produce of the Dan River valley. Until the Richmond and Danville Railroad was completed in 1856, enabling it to tap the valley at Danville, bateau voyages terminated at Weldon, which by 1833 was connected by rail to Petersburg. Goods shipped eastward by bateau as far as Weldon could also be placed aboard steamboats for transshipment to

Norfolk via the Dismal Swamp Canal. The Smith River, a tributary of the Dan, was improved by a Virginia-based navigation company in 1850-1851, but an untimely freshet damaged the works and repairs were never completed.

Rumors of the improvements in navigation and the actual work on the waterways touched off an economic boom in the Dan valley that persisted until the onset of the Panic of 1819, America's first national depression. Speculators ascended the river, ballyhooing various towns as the head of navigation and accumulating immense profits through land sales at inflated prices. Milton, Danville, and Leaksville were subjected to overpromotion, and new towns, which came to be known as Madison, Jackson, Jamestown, and Hairstonborough, were proposed.

The Barnett Era

A new era began in Leaksville in May, 1813, when James Barnett purchased a 2,912-acre tract of the old Farley estate for $8,600. Barnett, riding the inflationary wave of land speculation, expanded Leaksville, selling lots that had brought from $10.00 to $20.00 before 1800 for $75.00 to $100 each. A peak was achieved in 1818 when the price of half-acre lots soared from $500 to $1,500 within a period of one year. Sterling Ruffin, who purchased lots in Leaksville during this time, wrote in July, 1818, that Leaksville was growing so rapidly that a branch of the State Bank of North Carolina was being requested for the town; during the following year the branch was established.

With a view toward a possible future market, the county court in 1817 and 1818 appointed tobacco inspectors for Leaksville and also for the adjacent settlements at Jamestown and Hogtown. In Hogtown, a community on the Dan River at Leaksville landing, John Lenox received permission to open a tobacco warehouse. Additional evidence of the bustling activity in Leaksville was the large tavern erected by James Barnett and John Menzies, as well as the license granted to Philip Rose for a "house of entertainment." Members of the Morehead family were given permission to sell liquor in their blacksmith shop. Notable merchants in the town during this period were Fontaine, Gregory and Company and Nathaniel W. Dandridge, who later formed a partnership with Patrick H. Fontaine. John Lenox, Leaksville's earliest known postmaster, was appointed in 1822, although mail service probably began at an earlier date.

James Barnett, then a county justice, devoted much of his time, energy, and capital to the development of the Jamestown settlement at Island Ford on the Smith River. At a rapid north of the ford he erected a wooden dam and had a 4,200-foot canal dug to Island Ford, where he constructed a large gristmill with an overshot wheel. On a hill overlooking the site, the Barnetts built their homeplace, which stands at the present time in a much altered condition. By harnessing the power of the Smith River, the Barnetts initiated an industrial revolution in Leaksville, which would become an important factor affecting the future of the town. James Barnett eventually departed Leaksville and went to Kentucky, leaving the family interests in the hands of his cousin, William Barnett, Jr.

By 1831 William Barnett had formed a business partnership with John Motley Morehead, a Greensboro attorney who had grown up in Rockingham County on his father's farm southeast of Leaksville. The Barnett and Morehead firm was successful, and in 1836, when Morehead secured complete control of the business, it consisted of the Island Ford gristmill, a sawmill, an oil mill, a carding machine, a cotton gin, and a general store. By 1837 Morehead had formed a partnership with William A. Carrigan; the new firm continued to operate the industries in the Jamestown area and later a warehouse on Water Street in Leaksville.

The Founding of Madison

The town of Madison, situated near the confluence of the Dan and Mayo rivers, was founded as a potential river port during the economic boom that ensued at the close of the War of 1812. The General Assembly chartered the town in 1815 with Joshua Smith, Richard Wall, Nicholas Dalton, John Guy, and Joel Cardwell as the first commissioners. By 1818 Randal Duke Scales had acquired from his father, Peter Scales, 324 acres in the town and had surveyed 96 half-acre lots laid off on eight streets. At an auction held in June of that year, these town lots were sold at prices ranging from $67.00 to $100 each. The county court designated tobacco inspectors for Madison in the apparent belief that the new town would become a market center for the western part of the county.

Tobacco manufacturing became the core of the town's economy. In the antebellum period tobacco was usually processed on the farm by being pressed or twisted into plugs or ropes for chewing or shredded into smoking tobacco for use in pipes. The finished product was loaded onto farm wagons or carts and peddled in the Deep South and was often bartered for needed products. The earliest known tobacco-processing facility in Madison was a stemmery that existed during the 1830s on Academy Street behind the home of Joseph Twitchell, son-in-law of Randal Duke Scales; there stems were removed from cured tobacco leaves. During the 1840s James Webster, Nicholas Dalton, Pleasant Scales, John Walker, and William Scales erected plug-tobacco factories in Madison.

The Town of Jackson

In the big "bent" of the Dan River is a shallow rapid known as Eagle Falls, where a major ford, or river crossing, was located. Virginia promoters seized upon this site as a potential head of navigation on the river and purchased it from William Wray in April, 1818. These men divided the property into a number of lots and sold them at auction on April 15, 1818, for $500 each. By August the price had doubled; but the following year, when the town had not materialized, the prices were lower. The Panic of 1819 then commenced, and prices for the lots plummeted to $25.00 each; by August, 1819, a typical lot sold for $1.00.

The Panic of 1819 dealt a fatal blow to the young town of Jackson, which had been conceived in an atmosphere of expansionism and prosperity. In 1826 John Morehead brought suit to set aside a debt related to two lots in Jackson. Morehead alleged that the promoters of the ill-fated town had defrauded him. The state supreme court agreed with Morehead, ruling that although the company had not defrauded the purchasers of the lots, it had made exaggerated claims and used bid "puffers" to increase sales. An example of the methods used by the promoters is the following ditty, which was supposedly sung to the tune of "Yankee Doodle" on the day of the auction and remained popular on the river for years thereafter:

> Danville's drunk, Leaksville's sunk
> Hogtown's all on fire;
> Boats go up to Eagle Falls,
> But can't go any higher.
>
> So clear the way for Jackson Town,
> No others need aspire.
> She's got the coon and pretty soon
> She'll set the world on fire.

The Panic of 1819

As early as 1817 Archibald D. Murphey characterized the runaway speculation at Danville as "a Bubble and will soon burst." The bubble might have remained intact if the war-stimulated European demand for American cotton, wheat, and other agricultural products had not waned. But with commodity prices falling, banks began to call in their loans; this led to defaults and bank failures. In January, 1819, cotton sold on the Richmond market for 33 cents a pound; by June it was 20 cents; and when the harvest came in the autumn, the price fell to less than 20 cents. Just after the War of 1812 tobacco brought $20.00 to $40.00 per hundred pounds; but by June, 1819, it was selling for $4.00 to $8.00 per hundred. Wrote Sterling Ruffin in July, 1819: "In this section of Country, we are now borne down under the extreme pressure for money, but the distress experienced now, is nothing to what will be felt ere long." Even more pessimistic was a letter written from Wentworth by William Roane in November, 1819. "N. Carolina," Roane wrote, "is not a soil calculated either to Display Genius or to make a mans fortune when compaired with many parts of the U.S.... Everything both of a political and domestic nature is tinctured with Nigardlyness."

The Founding of Reidsville

Unrelated to the land boom in the Dan River valley but nevertheless important for the future of the county was the development of the village of Reidsville. William Wright (1762-1824), who resided at a plantation on Little Troublesome Creek, owned a tavern and store on the road that connected Danville and Salem. Wright called this outpost Wright's Cross Roads; it was the earliest settlement in the present city of Reidsville. By 1814 Wright had acquired property in Wentworth, where two years later he erected a tavern. Wright's son Nathan continued the family enterprise at Wright's Cross Roads. Nathan's son-in-law, Robert Payne Richardson, later became the family entrepreneur. The home built by the Richardsons in 1842 stands at the present time on a knoll overlooking Little Troublesome Creek and is the oldest standing house in Reidsville.

In May, 1814, Reuben Reid of the Hogan's Creek area moved his family to a 700-acre farm on the ridge between Wolf Island and Little Troublesome creeks. Two years earlier Reid had married Elizabeth Williams Settle, and on April 19, 1813, their first son, David Settle Reid, was born. David S. Reid would become the county's most important political figure of the nineteenth century. The Reids settled in a log house on the Danville road and soon opened a store and ordinary (a public inn maintained in a private home). Reuben Reid became a successful farmer and served the county as a constable and justice of the peace. In 1829 the Reids secured a post office, which was named Reidsville, and sixteen-year-old David Reid was appointed the first postmaster.

An 1826 Coach Trip

An interesting account of a journey by way of the road from Salem through Rockingham County was written by Charles A. Van Vleck, a Moravian clergyman who with his family passed through the county in October, 1826, en route by coach to Bethlehem, Pennsylvania. The Van Vlecks slept very comfortably at James Patrick's ordinary near Troublesome Creek Ironworks. The bill for supper and bed for the party of six, including the driver of the coach, and for care of the horses was $2.25.

On the following morning the Van Vlecks partook of "a most wretched" breakfast at Reid's ordinary. Resuming their trip, the family passed by the home and "entertainment" of William D. Bethel, who was then a brigadier general of militia; but the Van Vlecks chose instead to stay overnight in Caswell County. They had breakfast the following day at Bell Tavern in Danville. The journey from Salem had begun at three

The home and "entertainment" of William D. Bethel (1764-1834), a militia officer and member of the General Assembly, was located in the northeastern section of the county. It was popularly known as Bethel Castle. The structure is believed to have been destroyed by fire in 1933. Photograph from copy in North Carolina Collection.

o'clock in the afternoon of October 8, and the Van Vlecks arrived in Danville on the morning of October 11, having spent three nights on the road. The same trip today is a leisurely two-hour drive.

Westward Emigration

Rockingham County's population increased steadily throughout the antebellum period in spite of extensive emigration from the upper South to the newly opened and fertile cotton lands of Alabama, Mississippi, East Texas, and Missouri. The children of Abraham Philips, a leading early citizen of Rockingham County, settled in Alabama in the 1830s. In 1837 William M. Wall, a resident of the county, moved his family to Missouri, where he became a successful miller. The most extensive mass migration from the county to have been documented occurred in 1839 when 144 residents of the Sardis Church area gathered for the purpose of moving to Missouri. Randal Duke Scales, the founder of Madison, sold his plantation and moved to Mississippi in 1844. Descendants of these and many other emigrants from Rockingham County today seek and find clues to their family roots in the county's records and cemeteries.

The Mexican War

The Mexican War was generally popular among southerners, who had welcomed Texas into the Union as a new slave state. Rockingham County, true to its Democratic heritage, responded positively to President James K. Polk's expansionist policies and enthusiastically supported the war. In 1846 Patrick M. Henry, a teacher at the Leaksville Academy, raised a company of volunteers for service in Mexico. Henry had previously served in the army as a lieutenant in the Seminole War.

The company was formed following a patriotic rally in Leaksville. Henry was elected captain, and the lieutenants were Peter Scales and Joseph Martin. The unit was mustered into the First North Carolina Volunteer Regiment as Company G, and in February, 1847, the regiment, commanded by Colonel Robert T. Paine, departed Fort Johnston (Southport) aboard a vessel bound for Mexico. While at sea, Lieutenant Peter Scales became ill and died.

After arriving in Mexico, the regiment was assigned to General Zachary Taylor's army in the north. Taylor had won lasting fame (and would soon win the presidency) by his victories at Monterey and Buena Vista, but the principal military activity had shifted to the south, where General Winfield Scott had invaded Vera Cruz and eventually captured Mexico City. The North Carolina regiment, garrisoned at Saltillo, saw no action and was saddled with the onerous duty of guarding supplies. Morale plummeted, desertion increased, and disease and death stalked the regiment, resulting in the loss of one quarter of the men. In the Rockingham County company at least four men died. Colonel Paine, a martinet, finally triggered a mutiny, which was quashed by Captain Henry and other loyal officers.

Antebellum Politics

A new state constitution adopted by North Carolina in 1835 provided for the first time for the popular election of the governor and set the stage for an era of spirited two-party politics. The new Whig party became the principal advocate of a progressive program of state support for internal improvements, the establishment of banks, and balanced economic growth. It presented a marked contrast to the agrarian-minded Democrats, who were more concerned with preserving the status quo. The Whigs dominated state government after 1835, winning every gubernatorial election until 1850, when David S. Reid, running on the issue of "free suffrage" (elimination of a 50-acre qualification for senatorial suffrage), became the first popularly elected Democratic governor. During this period Rockingham County remained solidly Democratic, returning majorities of at least two to one in the various elections.

The county's Democrats provided capable leadership on the local, state, and national levels. George D. Boyd (1797-1886), a planter and merchant, served in the state House of Commons, 1840-1841, and in the state Senate, 1842-1847 and 1852-1859. Daniel W. Courts (1800-1883), an attorney, in addition to serving seven terms as a legislator, was state treasurer from 1836 to 1839 and from 1851 to 1862. Other Democratic legislators of this period were Dr. Thomas W. Keen; Francis L. Simpson, who also served as a major general in the state militia; Alfred M. Scales, who in 1856 was elected to the first of many terms in the United States House of Representatives; and Thomas Settle, Jr., who was elected

Speaker of the state House of Commons in 1858, thirty years after his father had held that post.

In spite of their status as a minority, Rockingham County's Whigs also produced able leaders who managed to win election to public office during the antebellum era. Dr. Edward T. Brodnax (1796-1874), the county's wealthiest planter, served two terms in the House of Commons, 1822-1824, and two terms in the state Senate, 1827-1829, and was elected a delegate to the 1835 and 1861-1862 state constitutional conventions.

Dr. Edward Travis Brodnax, a physician, wealthy planter, and prominent Whig, was elected to four terms in the North Carolina General Assembly and served as a delegate to two state constitutional conventions. Oil on canvas (1855) by William Garl Browne; photograph reproduced from Laura MacMillan (comp.), *The North Carolina Portrait Index, 1700-1860* (Chapel Hill: University of North Carolina Press, 1963), p. 32.

Robert Martin (1784-1848), a planter, served in the House of Commons from 1822 to 1826 and in the state Senate from 1829 to 1835, where he was a key advocate of a state bank. Martin was a brother-in-law of Thomas Settle, Sr. (1789-1857), an attorney and planter who served two terms in the United States House of Representatives, 1817-1821, and three terms as a member of the state House of Commons, 1826-1829. Settle was Speaker of the latter body from 1827 to 1829. In 1832 he was elected by the legislature to the state superior court, where he remained for twenty-one years, garnering a reputation as one of the state's most highly respected judges. John Motley Morehead, who was governor from 1841 to 1845, began his distinguished public career in the state House of Commons in 1821 as a representative from Rockingham County.

David S. Reid

Rockingham County's preeminent political leader of the antebellum period was David Settle Reid (1813-1891), whose distinguished career on the state and national levels spanned forty years. Largely self-educated and employed by the age of twelve, Reid won election in 1835 at the age of twenty-two to both the state Senate and to the colonelcy of the county militia regiment. After five years in the Senate, he was elected to two terms in the United States House of Representatives, 1843-1847, where he was an ardent spokesman for the Polk administration.

In Washington Reid met and formed a lifelong friendship with Stephen A. Douglas of Illinois. Reid introduced his attractive cousin,

37

David Settle Reid, the county's "preeminent political leader of the antebellum period." Oil on canvas (1850) by William Garl Browne; photograph from the files of the Division of Archives and History.

Martha Martin, to Douglas, and on April 7, 1847, the couple were married at the Martin plantation on the Dan River. The Douglas family lived in Chicago and Washington, but the sons of Stephen Douglas eventually returned to North Carolina, where his descendants still reside.

Reid lost his congressional seat through a Whig-engineered legislative gerrymander but was persuaded to run for governor in 1848 by William W. Holden, powerful editor of the Raleigh *North Carolina Standard*, the official state organ of the Democratic party. Reid was defeated by Whig Charles Manly by a margin of only 854 votes, the closest election in the state's history and a moral victory for the Democrats. Two years later Reid trounced Manly, shattering permanently the Whigs' hold on the state and ushering in the Democratic era, which has persisted with few interruptions until the present time. Reid won election to a term in the United States Senate, 1854-1859, and closed his political career by serving as a delegate to the state constitutional conventions of 1861-1862 and 1875.

A Political Dynasty

Through family and marriage ties the Reids, Settles, Martins, and Graveses constituted the most remarkable political dynasty in the state's history. Three children of David Settle made the key marriages in the dynasty: Thomas Settle, Sr., to Henrietta Graves; Elizabeth Settle to Reuben Reid; and Mary Settle to Robert Martin. Over three generations, the descendants of these unions and their in-laws produced a presidential candidate in 1860 (Stephen A. Douglas), two United States senators (Stephen Douglas and David S. Reid), four United States representatives (Douglas, Reid, Thomas Settle, Sr., and Thomas Settle III), a governor (Reid), two state supreme court justices (Thomas Settle, Jr., and Robert M. Douglas), and three Speakers of the state House of Commons (Thomas Settle, Sr., Thomas Settle, Jr., and Calvin

Graves). Few families in the nation and no other in the state can match the record of distinguished public service achieved by this family.

The "Six Governors" Myth

A cherished political myth connected with Rockingham County is that it nurtured six governors of North Carolina: Alexander Martin, who served as governor from 1782 to 1785 and again from 1789 to 1792, John Motley Morehead (1841-1845), David S. Reid (1851-1854), Alfred M. Scales (1885-1889), Robert B. Glenn (1905-1909), and Luther H. Hodges (1954-1961). While it is true that all six of these governors were connected in one way or another with Rockingham County, only two of them, Reid and Hodges, were elected to office at the time they resided in the county. Only one of them, Reid, was born in the county, lived there all of his life, and was buried there. Alexander Martin, a native of New Jersey, owned a plantation on the Dan River, to which he retired; but during his active political career his principal residence was at Guilford Courthouse. John M. Morehead, born in Virginia, grew up in Rockingham County and had extensive business interests in Leaksville, but his residence was in Greensboro. Alfred M. Scales was born in the county and resided in Madison and Wentworth until after the Civil War, at which time he moved to Greensboro. Robert B. Glenn, a native of the county, resided there until adulthood and also inherited property there; but his legal career and adult years were spent as a resident of Danbury and Winston-Salem. Luther H. Hodges was born in Pittsylvania County, Virginia, but his family moved to Leaksville when he was two years old.

The Plantation and Slavery

Rockingham County, like most of the South, prospered during the 1850s. The county's total population burgeoned from 14,495 in 1850 to 16,746 in 1860. During the same period the slave population increased from 5,329 to 6,318. There were 419 free blacks residing in the county in 1850 and 409 in 1860.

Annual production of the county's leading crop, tobacco, went from 1,777,205 pounds in 1850 to 3,158,333 pounds in 1860. In 1850 the county produced 431,085 bushels of corn, 149,402 bushels of oats, 61,015 bushels of wheat, 4,805 bushels of rye, 29,947 pounds of cotton, and 8,355 pounds of wool. A county agricultural society was organized in 1855, but nothing is known of its activities after the initial meeting.

No study of the county's antebellum farms and plantations has been undertaken, but several examples can furnish information about typical farm products. James Wright, a Wentworth innkeeper, operated a 750-acre farm on Rockhouse Creek. In 1860 he maintained 100 acres of improved land and owned twenty-four slaves. The farm produced 5,500 pounds of tobacco, 1,125 bushels of corn, 15 tons of hay, and small quantities of wheat, oats, peas, wool, potatoes, yams, butter, wine, molasses, and honey. Wright owned 5 horses, a mule, 5 milch cows, 7 head of cattle, 10 sheep, and 10 hogs. Just a few miles northwest of Wentworth was David S. Reid's 700-acre Dan River plantation, which had been a wedding gift from his father-in-law, Thomas Settle, when Reid married his first cousin, Henrietta Settle. Reid had improved 300 acres of his farm by 1860, at which time he harvested 7,000 pounds of tobacco, 1,250 bushels of corn, 215 bushels of wheat, 200 bushels of oats, 100 bushels of yams, 50 bushels of potatoes, and 5 bushels of peas. Reid's livestock in 1860 consisted of 3 horses, 3 mules, 6 milch cows, 4 head of cattle, and 43 hogs. Some of the stock was slaughtered for meat, and the cows produced 200 pounds of butter during that year.

The majority of the county's farmers owned few or no slaves and worked fewer than 200 acres. Thomas J. Worsham, who resided near Ruffin in 1860, owned one slave and 154 acres of land from which he harvested 28 bushels of wheat, 150 bushels of corn, and 3,000 pounds of tobacco. He owned 2 horses, 3 cows, 5 sheep, and 14 hogs. In the Spring Garden (Shiloh) area Wilford Carter owned 56 acres of land but no slaves in 1860. The products of his farm included 100 bushels of wheat, 180 bushels of corn, 100 bushels of oats, 2,250 pounds of tobacco, 15 bushels of Irish potatoes, 5 pounds of flax, and 150 pounds of butter. His livestock consisted of a horse, 2 milch cows, 2 head of cattle, 3 sheep, and 14 hogs.

Slaves represented the primary labor source on the larger plantations and also supplemented the labor of family members on small farms. David Reid owned twenty-two slaves in 1860, but half of them were children eleven years old or younger. Thomas Roach (1797-1860), a county justice, accumulated 800 acres of creek bottom and ridge land on the north fork of Wolf Island Creek and owned twenty slaves. The largest slaveholder in the county in 1860 was Dr. Edward T. Brodnax, who worked 174 slaves on 5,000 acres, much of his land being prime Dan River bottomland. The average age of Rockingham County slaves in 1860, according to one random sampling, was twenty. Most slave families included a number of children.

Two of the county's slave traders were R. G. Hopper of Leaksville and Anselom Reid, who was also a peddler. Reid circulated throughout the region with his coffle of slaves, selling them to various slave owners. He was active during the 1840s, and from his records slave values can be ascertained. In 1840 a nineteen-year-old man brought $750; the following year a thirteen-year-old girl was sold for $475; in 1844 a woman of fifty-four was worth only $75; but in the same year Reid received $600 for a group of slaves—two girls under nine years of age and two boys under the age of five.

Some planters lived in commodious two-story brick or frame homes, while small farmers usually resided in log houses or small frame structures. On his Dan River plantation Thomas S. Gallaway erected a large two-story brick manor, and a few miles upstream stood the frame house of Governor David S. Reid and the residence (completed in 1860) of Reid's cousin, Thomas Settle, Jr. The plantation house of Thomas Roach, erected in 1828 on Wolf Island Creek, was a one-and-one-half-story log house with massive stone chimneys. The structure's two original log rooms were joined by a frame shed. The Robert Courts house, a small one-and-one-half-story frame cottage just north of Reidsville, was the seat of still another upland plantation.

Antebellum Towns and Villages

A map of North Carolina drawn in 1808 reveals that Rockingham County had settlements at Wentworth, Leaksville, Sauratown, Danbury (Alexander Martin's plantation), Rocky Springs, and Rockingham Springs. The map also shows a number of individual farms. A government survey of 1865 lists many towns and crossroad villages in the

Shown above are the Rockingham County portions of the Price-Strother map of 1808 (left) and the United States Coast Survey of 1865 (right). Price-Strother map held by Library of Congress; coast survey held by Division of Archives and History; both reproduced courtesy of the Division.

county: Leaksville, Leaksville Factory, Wentworth, Reidsville, Lawson-ville, Rawlinsburg (Ruffin), Troublesome, Monroeton, Thompsonville, Oregon, Dan River, Eagle Falls, Elm Grove, Mayo (Stoneville), Ayers-ville, Madison, Pleasantville, Grogansville, Rockingham Springs, and High Rock. All of these places were designated as post offices at various times. Most of these post offices were located in a store and were usually accompanied by a house or two but little else. The only towns of significant size were Leaksville, Wentworth, and Madison, and even these were mere villages with only a few hundred inhabitants.

The Coming of Textiles

John Motley Morehead, a resident of Greensboro, had been involved in business interests in Leaksville that stemmed from his own enterprises

41

and from his earlier partnerships with William Barnett and William A. Carrigan. By 1836 Morehead owned the canal and mills on the Smith River and warehouses and a store in Leaksville. To his enterprising mind it was obvious that the canal was capable of supplying more waterpower than was then being utilized, so he decided to erect a textile mill. In 1839 he secured the services of John Hall Bullard (1808-1870) of Massachusetts, who apparently had been a textile mechanic, to build and manage his mill. Within a year a multistory stone building was erected to house the factory. In close proximity to it, on the low hills surrounding Tackett Branch, Morehead constructed a tenement for the mill's workers and brick houses for its managers. For his own use during his frequent visits from Greensboro, Morehead built a small brick cottage that overlooked the little valley. This structure, which evolved into the elegant Morehead-Mebane mansion, stood until recent years. Bullard eventually left the factory, went into business as a merchant in Leaksville, and built a home on Washington Street (which his descendants have preserved).

Morehead's mill, known as Leaksville Factory, initially produced cotton yarn; however, within a few years a weaving operation was added. In 1857 the mill converted 350,000 pounds of cotton into 120,000 yards of osnaburg, 150,000 yards of sheeting or shirting, and 240 pounds of yarn. The census of 1860 reveals that the factory provided employment for 25 men and 80 women and was capitalized at $70,000. The mill eventually was capable of processing wool.

A mill document of 1845 illustrates the extent to which barter was part of the antebellum economy. Anselom Reid purchased from the

Leaksville Factory, later known as Leaksville Cotton Mill, was erected for John Motley Morehead about 1840. In the foreground of this later view of the structure is the canal used by Morehead to power the mill. Photograph from *State*, XVI (November 6, 1948), p. 4.

Leaksville Factory forty bunches of cotton yarn valued at $31.38 and paid for it with 31 pounds of beeswax valued at $7.75, 17 pounds of feathers worth $4.25, 70 pounds of bacon valued at $5.60, 13¼ yards of flax cloth at $2.38, and $11.40 in cash. The factory commissary or store converted the beeswax into candles and sold the feathers for use in pillows or comforters.

In 1859 the *Fayetteville Observer* published a letter it had received from a recent visitor to the Leaksville Factory complex. The writer described the Morehead concern as

a large stone building . . . constructed in the most substantial manner, and of the most durable materials. It is situated at the mouth of a magnificent canal, leading from Smith's river, and operated by the largest and finest metal wheel that I have ever seen. Near by are the oil mills, flour mills, and saw mills—all operated by the water of the same canal, which appears to have a fall of at least 25 feet. . . .

Antebellum Business and Industry

By 1840 the leading industry in Rockingham County was tobacco manufacturing. The industry was centered in the town of Madison, but factories existed throughout the county. At that time 160 people were employed in processing tobacco. Other important industries were wagon and carriage manufacturing, which provided work for 85 people, and John M. Morehead's cotton factory, which employed 40 people. The county then boasted 36 gristmills, 25 sawmills, 13 flour mills, 5 tanneries, 2 oil mills, a furniture factory, and various firms engaged in the production of items such as iron, lime, brick, straw bonnets, caps and hats, and saddles and leather goods. Typical in the county were the small industrial complexes found near sources of waterpower. Clustered about the gristmill at High Rock on the Haw River were a sawmill, an oil mill, a cotton gin, and a cooper's shop.

In 1860 the county had 25 tobacco factories that together provided employment for 375 people. Rockingham then had more tobacco factories than any other county, but the factories were smaller, employed fewer people, and produced smaller quantities of tobacco. In 1858 William Lindsey of Reidsville had initiated production of a plug tobacco known as Lindsey's Level Best; nevertheless, Reidsville, the future center of tobacco manufacturing, was then little more than a post office and way station.

Daniel E. Field (1831-1916), a local minister and merchant, wrote a series of historical sketches that were published in the *Leaksville Gazette* in 1901 and provide excellent information concerning antebellum life in Leaksville. Field recounted that in 1840 Leaksville consisted of three small stores, a wagon shop, a blacksmith shop, a tailor shop, and two whiskey shops. During the 1850s the town prospered, becoming the trade center for a large volume of backcountry produce.

Improvements by the Roanoke Navigation Company had made the Dan River navigable to the extent that steam navigation was being considered. The river port thrived with goods coming from as far west as the Blue Ridge Mountains in Virginia.

Field noted Leaksville's important commercial connection with Lynchburg, Virginia, which could be reached overland by freight wagons or horse-drawn wooden hogsheads filled with tobacco. He described Barney Cahal, a colorful teamster who utilized a five-horse wagon to haul 3,000 pounds of freight between the two towns, charging a fee of $1.25 per hundred pounds of cargo. The round trip to Lynchburg normally took ten days. Local teamsters also hitched hogsheads of tobacco to teams of horses and drove them to the Lynchburg market.

Robert Ward founded the Leaksville *Herald,* the town's first newspaper, in 1860. Advertisements that appear in the few surviving issues of the journal give some indication of the commercial activity in the town. General merchants in 1860-1861 included J. H. Bullard and J. B. Ray, M. J. Hampton, Jones W. Burton, and Pryor Reynolds. Local craftsmen were James R. Stephens, a cabinetmaker; Peter D. Wade, a harness maker; J. L. Callahan, a shoemaker; Benton J. Field, a jeweler; and T. H. Morgan, a producer of ambrotype portraits. An industrial complex existed nearby on Matrimony Creek, where in 1860 Thomas A. Ragland operated a gristmill, a foundry, a cabinet shop, and a tanyard.

John Hall Bullard, described by Daniel Field as Leaksville's "pioneer modern merchant," secured goods in the North, introduced new products locally and undersold his competitors. According to Field, Bullard was the first merchant in Leaksville to sell oil lamps, improved matches, carriage bolts, gimlet-pointed wooden screws, wooden shoe pegs, figured corduroy, men's clothing, and a sugar mill. Daniel Arney, a competitor of Bullard, manufactured tallow and sperm-oil candles at the rate of a dozen thirty-pound boxes per day.

Madison, benefiting from the improved Dan River navigation, grew steadily during the 1850s. Local merchants were Jordan and Connor, John M. Rose, Calvin N. MacAdoo, and the McGehee family. There were two tinsmiths in the village, Milton Stamps and James Churchill. John New was a shoemaker. Madison also boasted a cabinetmaker, a tanner, a horse doctor, a physician, a harness maker, a printer, a druggist, and a daguerreotypist. In 1857 William L. Sneed purchased the press of the *Rockingham Democrat* (which had been established by 1855) and began the Madison *Weekly News.*

Academies and Private Schools

Prior to the nineteenth century, education was a personal matter. Available to the wealthy were private tutors or academies, but the poor had virtually no educational opportunities. Basic education was provided in the home, if at all, or several families might hire a teacher to conduct a small private school for a few months. Classical academies, the secondary schools of the day, concentrated on Greek, Latin, rhetoric, grammar, and mathematics. Only one academy existed in the Rockingham County area during this period; it was conducted in Guilford County by the Reverend David Caldwell from 1767 to 1824, and the sons of a few local planters attended this school. A typical plantation school was located at the home of Judge Thomas Settle just east of Reidsville; the school was housed in a small brick building that survived until recent years.

In 1820 the county's first classical academies opened in Leaksville and Madison. The Leaksville Academy was advertised in the Raleigh *Star* in January, 1820. For a tuition of $30.00 the instructor, John Silliman, offered a course in Latin, Greek, English, and science. Through the academy Silliman concurrently offered an elementary course in reading, writing, and arithmetic for $20.00. A library and a debating society enriched the curriculum. Boarding students could find space in town for $8.00 to $12.00 per month.

In February, 1820, James Barnett, to "promote literature and learning," conveyed to the trustees of the Leaksville Male Academy a lot on Henry Street for $1.00. The twenty-seven trustees were some of the county's most prominent citizens. A two-story brick building was erected to house the school, the lower story of which presently stands in a modified form on the original site. Daniel Field noted that in 1839 there existed in Leaksville a male academy directed by Patrick M. Henry and a female academy conducted by Miss Charlotte Jennings of New York, who later married John Lawson, a town merchant.

An advertisement in the *Raleigh Register* announced that the Madison Academy would open its doors on July 4, 1820. The school opened in a log building on Academy Street. The trustees employed James F. Martin, a graduate of the state university, to teach a classical course. Students could board in the town for $30.00. In 1844 a frame structure replaced the log building, and Henry Baughn conducted the school. In the 1850s the school was renamed the Beulah Academy; Lewis H. Shook, a Baptist minister, taught there from 1858 to 1872.

North Carolina's public school system was established under a law enacted in 1839, and the first public school in the state was opened in the Williamsburg area of Rockingham County on January 20, 1840. Unfortunately, the precise location of this school is not known. Under the law the schools were to operate for a term of at least two and one half months, for which teachers were paid $20.00 in county funds and $40.00 in state funds. The county provided the building—usually a rude log hut. The 1848 report of the county school chairman, John L. Lesueur, enumerated thirty-five school districts and thirty-nine teachers. At that time only one woman, Isabella M. Harris, taught in the county. School terms averaged five months, for which a salary of $74.12½ was paid. The total educational budget for the county in 1848 was $2,706.20.

Numa F. Reid, a graduate of Emory and Henry College, opened a school at Salem Church near Wentworth in 1843. Alberta R. Craig, who later taught in this school, apparently in the original building, recalled that the "benches were made of split logs and had no backs. The room was heated by an immense open fireplace, and the writing-desk was a long polished board that extended across the back of the room, under the main window. The children's classes ranged all the way from the first to the seventh grade. The school lasted four months." In 1844 Numa Reid and Franklin Harris opened the first academy in the town of Wentworth. The following year Reid alone conducted the school, continuing it until 1849 when he entered the ministry.

In 1855 Marinda Branson Moore opened Margarita Seminary near her home on Belews Creek. For this school she created the Dixie Readers, a series of textbooks published by her brother Levi Branson and used extensively in the region.

The Antebellum Churches

The Presbyterian church entered a new era of growth in the nineteenth century. Spring Garden, the mother church of the Madison and Leaksville congregations, was organized as early as 1832 with Thompson Bird as minister. In 1838 Nathaniel Scales donated to the church a lot in the present Shiloh community, on which a building was constructed. The church was originally named Leaksville Presbyterian, but in 1837 the name was changed to Spring Garden; William N. Mebane was its pastor by 1840.

The inconvenience of traveling several miles to reach the church prompted members of the congregation who resided in Madison to withdraw from Spring Garden and organize a separate congregation; in 1851 the new congregation erected the building presently occupied by the Madison Presbyterian Church. William N. Mebane was the first

This building, erected in 1851, was later occupied by the congregation of the Madison Presbyterian Church. Photograph courtesy Special Collections, Rockingham Community College Library, Wentworth.

pastor, serving until 1859, and other leading ministers of this period were Pleasant H. Dalton and B. Watt Mebane.

The Leaksville Presbyterian Church was organized in 1860 from the remnant of the Spring Garden congregation, and a building, which stands at the present time, was erected in 1880. The first pastor was the Reverend John W. Montgomery.

In 1859 the Wentworth Presbyterian Church was organized by the Reverend Donald E. Jordan. The following year Colonel James Irvin, a trustee, purchased for the church the old jail lot, on which the present building was soon erected.

An era of dissension and division in the Baptist church was also one of unprecedented growth for the denomination. Differences on matters affecting missionary societies, church schools, conventions, and an educated ministry developed among the various congregations. During the formative period of the Baptist presence in the county, each congregation made its own decisions. Over the years attitudes became rigid, and by the 1830s a major split developed on the question of whether a Baptist state convention should be established. In 1833 the Country Line Association, which embodied all of Rockingham County's Baptist congregations, condemned the notion of a convention; as a result, several churches left the association the following year. Members of these congregations, who came to refer to themselves as missionary Baptists, organized the Beulah Association under the leadership of Stephen Pleasant.

Two missionaries of the Beulah Association, John Robertson and Elias Dodson, did more to expand the Baptist church in Rockingham County than anyone else. The indefatigable Robertson (1804-1880), a native of the county, founded churches at Leaksville, Madison, Hogan's Creek, and Elm Grove. Dodson (ca. 1807-1882), a Virginian and graduate of the College of William and Mary, was an itinerant minister in the area for many years.

In August, 1841, John Robertson gathered the many Baptists in Leaksville and organized a congregation, which met initially in the academy building. In November of that year Robertson and Dodson organized the Madison congregation, which erected a building in 1850. The first pastor in Madison was John M. New. In 1843 Robertson established the Hogan's Creek Baptist Church.

The Methodists, who were already well established in the countryside, came to the towns during this period. The Leaksville Methodist Church was organized in 1837 as part of the Virginia Conference and entered the North Carolina Conference in 1845. Benton Field, a former minister, was an able lay leader in this congregation. By 1859 the Methodists were sharing a two-story frame building on Jay Street with the Masons.

In January, 1843, Randal Duke Scales deeded a town lot to the newly formed Madison Methodist Church. By 1845 this congregation occupied a frame building that until recent years stood adjacent to the old town cemetery.

The oldest Methodist church building in the county is in Wentworth. The church was organized in 1836, and the building, which stands at the present time in an excellent state of preservation, was erected in 1859. Two noted Methodist ministers associated with this church were Numa F. Reid and Frank Lewis Reid (1851-1894), sons of the Reverend James Reid of Mount Carmel. Numa Reid opened a school in Wentworth, married Ann E. Wright, daughter of James Wright, and frequently preached at the Methodist church. After only two years in the ministry Frank Reid became editor of the *North Carolina Christian Advocate*, a Methodist newspaper, and later served as president of Louisburg College and then Greensboro College.

The colonial Anglican church was disestablished during the American Revolution, and many former Anglicans apparently became Methodists. Rockingham County's first Episcopal church, the Church of the Epiphany, was organized in Leaksville in 1844. That same year Dr. Edward T. Brodnax donated a tract of land as a site for the present building, and the structure was dedicated the following year.

Bridges, Steamboats, and Railroads

During the nineteenth century the Dan River, which traversed the county and was impassable when flooded, was bridged at Madison, Leaksville, and Dead Timber Ford above Eagle Falls. The two earliest bridges were erected during the 1830s at Madison and Leaksville by private companies, which constructed toll bridges at the sites of earlier fords or ferries. During the latter part of the century a covered bridge replaced the Madison Toll Bridge, whose existence was lost to history until the recent discovery of a piece of currency issued by the company that operated it.

The Leaksville Toll Bridge Company erected a bridge over the Dan River in 1833. It served the town until August, 1850, when a freshet

This demand note in the amount of $1.00 was issued ca. 1833 by the proprietors of the Madison Toll Bridge. Photograph courtesy Madison Historic Properties Commission.

swept it away. The structure figured in the 1846 murder of a clerk named Victor Lewis. Lewis was found shot to death in a store, and the store's strongbox had been robbed of 13 cents. The murderer, one Thomas G. Ellington, was later identified in part by a witness who had noted the peculiar gait of Ellington's horse as it crossed the bridge shortly after the time of the murder. Ellington was publicly hanged in Wentworth on May 21, 1847, and confessed his crime on the gallows.

The toll bridge company later hired a contractor to replace the old bridge, and the new one, with a latticed cover, was completed in 1852. The new structure was operated as a toll bridge until the county purchased it in 1886. The tollkeeper, who lived on the Leaksville road near the bridge, collected a toll of 10 cents for each vehicle that crossed the structure. The bridge remained in use until, weakened by age and neglect, it collapsed in 1943. The massive hewn stone pier and south abutment stand at the present time, dominating the river at the site. In 1854 a wooden truss bridge was completed across the Smith River at Island Ford near the Morehead factory.

In 1850 a freshet washed out a bridge at Eagle Falls. This structure was replaced at least once before 1870, at which time a new location, upriver at Dead Timber Ford, was chosen as the site of a covered span that came to be known as Settle's Bridge. This bridge was in use by 1875 and spanned the Dan River until 1952, when the State Highway Commission ordered that it be replaced.

Settle's Bridge was originally erected in 1870 to span the Dan River. After being damaged by a flood the span was rebuilt in 1875 and remained extant until 1952. The 1875 structure is pictured here. Photograph from Capus Waynick, *North Carolina Roads and Their Builders* (Raleigh: Superior Stone Company, 1952), p. 25.

In the era before the Civil War the Dan River navigation system was utilized extensively as a means of floating tobacco downstream to markets in Virginia and to bring goods into the upper Dan valley. Leaksville became the hub of this backcountry commerce. By 1852 the *Lily of the Dan*, a steamboat owned by Dr. T. L. Sydnor of Danville, was making the run between Leaksville and Madison. The trip upriver took two days and the return trip one day. The vessel may have been used only for excursions, or it might have been utilized as a towboat for bateaux. In

1855 the Dan River Steam Navigation Company was incorporated in North Carolina for the purpose of operating a commercial towboat on the river. Whether or not this company actually operated a vessel is not known, but evidence suggests that there was a commercial steamboat on the river by 1874.

John M. Morehead, president of the North Carolina Railroad Company, had long sought a rail connection from Danville through Leaksville to Greensboro. In 1858, with Morehead's support, Francis L. Simpson, a member of the state House of Commons, launched an effort to win legislative sanction of a rail line to run through Rockingham County. Many legislators believed that such a road, which was to connect with the existing Richmond & Danville Railroad, would merely serve to enrich Virginia at the expense of North Carolina, and an acrimonious battle ensued in the General Assembly. Nevertheless, on February 16, 1859, the legislature chartered the Dan River & Coalfields Railroad, which was to extend from Danville to Leaksville, and construction contracts were let the following year. In November, 1860, the Greensboro & Leaksville Railroad was chartered, but the onset of the Civil War doomed both of these projects. During the war the Confederate government intervened to link Greensboro and Danville by a more direct rail route through the eastern part of Rockingham County.

V. THE CIVIL WAR ERA

The Civil War

In general, North Carolinians viewed with apprehension the secession of the southern states, which led to four years of bloody conflict and the destruction of the plantation South. Not until the firing on Fort Sumter in April, 1861, and President Abraham Lincoln's call for troops did the state join the Confederacy. Rockingham County, like the state as a whole, had awarded a majority of its votes to proslavery Democrat John C. Breckinridge of Kentucky in the presidential election of 1860. The more moderate Stephen A. Douglas, despite his local ties, had trailed a poor third in both the county and the state. In a statewide election held in February, 1861, for the purpose of selecting delegates to attend a convention to consider secession, a majority of the successful candidates were Unionists. Elected from Rockingham County were Dr. Edward T. Brodnax, a Whig Unionist who, though opposed to secession, agreed to abide by the will of the majority, and Thomas Settle, a Democrat. Former governor David S. Reid, by then an elder statesman of the Democratic party and a moderate secessionist, was appointed one of five delegates to represent the state at the Washington Peace Conference of February, 1861, which ultimately failed to achieve a compromise.

At a rally held in Wentworth on April 24 for the purpose of raising volunteers for defense of the state, the speakers were former governor Reid, John M. Gallaway, Alfred M. Scales, John H. Dillard, Thomas Settle, Jr., and Numa F. Reid. Numa Reid recorded in his diary that "we have been Union men—have done all we could honorably do to save the Union. I would rejoice if we could remain United, but we are compelled to yield now. We must either fight our own Governor and State authorities or fight President Lincoln, and we have chosen the latter."

The drama of the coming crisis was felt deeply by those destined to become participants. R. S. Williams, who served as captain of Company I, Thirteenth Regiment North Carolina Troops, later recalled that "When the State of North Carolina seceded everything was in a commotion and excitement ran high. . . . The fife and drum could be heard in every town and at every crossroads in Rockingham county."

In May, 1861, the county court, anticipating secession, appropriated $25,000 to outfit volunteers for the war and support their families during their absence. The state seceded on May 20, and the court established a military central committee for the county. Rockingham County supplied a total of 1,711 men for the Confederate army, not including the Senior Reserves. Most of the men were members of the Thirteenth and

Forty-fifth regiments, although local companies also served in the Fourteenth, Twenty-first, and Sixty-third (Fifth Cavalry) regiments and in the Junior Reserves.

Alfred M. Scales rose during the war to the rank of brigadier general and was the highest-ranking officer from Rockingham County. A native of the county, Scales was educated at the University of North Carolina and in 1851 began law practice in Madison, where his original law office is preserved. The Thirteenth Regiment joined the Army of Northern Virginia, and on October 11, 1861, Scales was elected colonel of the regiment. The regiment saw its first action in the Peninsula Campaign on May 5 at Williamsburg and was later engaged in the various actions of the Seven Days' battles. Scales fought at Fredericksburg and Chancellorsville, where he was wounded in the leg.

Alfred Moore Scales (1827-1892) served as a brigadier general in the Confederate army and was Rockingham County's highest-ranking Civil War officer. Photograph from Archibald Henderson, *North Carolina: The Old North State and the New* (Chicago: Lewis Publishing Company, 2 volumes, 1941), II, p. 253.

After recovering from his wounds, Scales was promoted to brigadier general on June 13, 1863. At Gettysburg in the first day's engagement on Seminary Ridge, he was again wounded. His brigade was ordered to take the ridge by frontal assault. After the battle Scales wrote that his men had "encountered a most terrific fire of grape and shell on our flank, and grape and musketry in our front. Every discharge made sad havoc in our line, but still we pressed on at a double-quick. . . ." In this attack the brigade suffered over 400 casualties. The Thirteenth Regiment lost 150 of its 180 men. Among the thirty survivors were two officers, Robert L. Moir and N. S. Smith. The regiment, supplemented by fifteen replacements, participated on July 3 in the great assault on Cemetery Ridge, which resulted in the loss of twenty-three men, leaving a total of twenty-two. General Scales returned to his brigade after recuperation, served in the campaigns of 1864, and was on convalescent leave at the end of the war.

Other high-ranking officers from Rockingham County were Samuel H. Boyd and John R. Winston, both of whom commanded the Forty-fifth Regiment, and Andrew J. Boyd, who was a lieutenant colonel in the unit. Thomas Ruffin, Jr., who was lieutenant colonel of the Thirteenth Regiment, commanded it at the battle of South Mountain, Virginia. Samuel H. Boyd, wounded and captured at Gettysburg, was later exchanged and rejoined the regiment just prior to the Battle of Spottsylvania Court House, during which he was killed on May 19, 1864. John R. Winston, who succeeded Boyd as the regimental commander, was likewise wounded and captured at Gettysburg. He was imprisoned on Johnson's Island in Lake Erie but escaped across the ice to Canada during the winter of 1863. He then went to Nassau in the Bahamas and returned to the war by way of a blockade-runner through Wilmington.

In the Twenty-first Regiment, Company L was organized in Wentworth on June 3, 1861, and joined the regiment at Danville on June 26. This company was commanded by John Hill Boyd, who died in Richmond in August, probably of an illness. He was succeeded by his brother, Andrew J. Boyd, who commanded the company until he was transferred to the Forty-fifth Regiment and promoted to major and later lieutenant colonel. Another Boyd brother, George F. Boyd, was a lieutenant in the Forty-fifth Regiment and was killed at Gettysburg. Three of the Boyd brothers—Samuel, John, and George—were buried by their father, George D. Boyd, in the Wentworth Methodist Cemetery.

Captain John Marion Gallaway, who was twice seriously wounded, commanded Company D of the Fifth North Carolina Cavalry (Sixty-third Regiment), known as the Rockingham Rangers. Also serving in this unit was James Turner Morehead, who was severely wounded at Bristoe Station, Virginia, in October, 1863. Gallaway was promoted to regimental major, and Morehead became the regimental adjutant. The Fifth Cavalry served briefly in eastern North Carolina and then joined the Army of Northern Virginia in May, 1863. The unit participated in numerous battles and skirmishes.

In a historical sketch of his regiment written in 1901, Major Gallaway contrasted the Union and Confederate equipment by reporting that the Confederate trooper was advised to discard his government issue and "wait till a battle gave him a chance to get 'something worth totin'.' " Gallaway noted that the Confederate "saddle ruined a horse's back, the canteen leaked, the haversack of cotton cloth was no protection, the English carbine was muzzle-loading and would not carry a ball fifty yards accurately. . . . It was a certain sign of a new recruit to see him with any article of Confederate equipment about him."

Both the Thirteenth and Forty-fifth regiments compiled impressive war records. In addition to the engagements already mentioned, the Thirteenth distinguished itself at South Mountain, Virginia, on September 14, 1862, during the Antietam campaign. Surrounded by Union forces, the regiment repeatedly, under heavy fire, changed its front, charged, repulsed the Federal troops, and re-formed. After being decimated at Gettysburg the revived regiment participated in the battles of the Wilderness, Spottsylvania Court House, Cold Harbor, and

Petersburg. Its survivors surrendered at Appomattox. Captain R. S. Williams took the members of his company to Danville, where they boarded a freight train and rode on top of the cars to Reidsville; there the war ended for them at the local depot at midnight.

The Forty-fifth Regiment saw as much action in the Army of Northern Virginia as the Thirteenth. Its baptism by fire came on June 30, 1862, in the battle of Frazier Farm. The green troops were loading their weapons in preparation for entering battle when a Union field battery opened fire, enfilading the line; a nearby Confederate cavalry squadron stampeded down upon them; and two Union gunboats with 160-pound cannon opened fire. Sergeant Cyrus Watson later wrote that "This was . . . a poor way to break in a raw regiment. The regiment thought so, and eight companies immediately broke to the woods. . . ." The companies under the command of Captains John W. May and John H. Dillard disappeared quickly but soon returned with Captain May's explanation that they had misunderstood their orders. Colonel Junius Daniel replied, "Yes, Captain, I saw the companies march up the lane at a very rapid gait, and, if I am not mistaken, their two Captains were making good time, and in front." The entire regiment, including the red-faced captains, broke into laughter.

The Forty-fifth regiment rapidly became a veteran unit. Following severe losses at Gettysburg, Daniel, then a brigadier general, declared that "Rockingham County has reason to be proud of the record made by the regiment at Gettysburg." In 1864 the regiment saw heavy fighting at the Wilderness, Spottsylvania, in the Valley of Virginia, and at Petersburg.

Several county physicians made significant contributions to Confederate medical service. John G. Brodnax (1829-1907), a native of Virginia, married his cousin, Mary W. Brodnax of Cascade plantation, and moved to the county in 1856. He had studied at the Medical College of Virginia and in Paris. He was commissioned as a surgeon in 1862 and supervised hospitals in Petersburg. The following year he was named director of the North Carolina hospitals in Petersburg. At the end of the war he was in charge of hospitals in Greensboro. Thomas W. Keen of Leaksville served briefly as surgeon of the Twenty-first Regiment, and Anthony B. Johns of Leaksville, John R. Raine of Wentworth, and William J. Courts, whose family lived north of Reidsville, served as surgeons in the Forty-fifth Regiment.

The most important event of the Civil War in Rockingham County was the construction of a railroad between Danville and Greensboro, which closed the only gap in a rail line that connected Virginia and the Deep South. Until this road was completed, Confederate troops moving northward or southward by rail had to be shunted either through eastern North Carolina or west of the Blue Ridge Mountains. At the urging of President Jefferson Davis, the Confederate Congress chartered the Piedmont Railroad Company early in 1862. The strategic needs of the Confederacy required that the railroad be completed as soon as possible; therefore, when Captain Edmund T. D. Myers of the Confederate Engineers surveyed for the line, he followed the most direct route—along a ridge in the eastern part of the county and through Reidsville. The Richmond & Danville Railroad Company acquired a controlling interest in the Piedmont Railroad, and the Confederate army supervised its construction. Contracts were let in May, 1862, and initial track laying proceeded from Danville; additional construction was later begun on the Greensboro end. So important was this rail link that Confederate troops and supplies were moved by train as far along the route as the work in progress would permit and then either marched or driven by wagon over the gap. The last section of track was laid in May, 1864. But even before the line was completed, Confederate rolling stock had deteriorated to the extent that the 50-mile trip took five hours. The Richmond & Danville Railroad Company retained the Piedmont Railroad after the war, and in 1894 it became part of the new Southern Railway System.

Letters written home by soldiers from the county reveal that the optimism expressed during the first year of the war gradually faded in light of illness, combat experiences, lack of food, and death to a realization that the war was lost. Although Union troops did not invade the county during the war, the population suffered the privations inflicted upon the Confederacy by shortages of commodities, high taxes, and inflation. Following Robert E. Lee's surrender at Appomattox, many Confederate soldiers passed through Leaksville on their way to their homes. Daniel Field, whose sketches vividly described local conditions at the end of the war, wrote that

Large bodies of soldiers, hungry and tired, were constantly passing [Leaksville] day and night, for ten days or more, until it was estimated eight or ten thousand had passed. . . . Tables were spread in the old Dillard porch and adjacent buildings and supplies of vegetables, meats and nick-nacks, with great quantities of butter milk, were placed upon these tables; while our noble women, old and young, gave them a hearty welcome from six in the morning until nine at night.

Reconstruction Politics and Government

During the bitter postwar era Rockingham County did not experience the racial-political revolution that transpired temporarily in other sections of the state. This is due at least in part to the fact that blacks historically have constituted only about 20 percent of the county's total population. The county remained true to its Democratic heritage, although a few prominent Republicans did gain public office. In 1865-1866 the county was represented at a state constitutional convention by Thomas Settle, Jr., soon to be a Republican leader, and Robert H. Ward, attorney and publisher of Leaksville. The county's delegates to an 1868 convention, which rewrote the state constitution, were Henry Barnes and John French.

The 1868 constitution altered county government significantly. It abolished the old appointed county courts and established in their place elected five-member boards of commissioners. The old captain's districts, utilized as geographical subdivisions for militia organization and tax collection, were replaced by townships that were to be governed by a town clerk and justices of the peace and to include a local school committee. Townships, so widely utilized in the North, never became meaningful governmental entities in the county and exist today only as administrative districts. The seven original townships in the county presently number eleven: Leaksville, Wentworth, Madison, Mayo, Price, Ruffin, Williamsburg, Reidsville, Huntsville, Simpsonville, and New Bethel. Under the state constitution of 1868 town government was organized by municipal corporation.

The first board of county commissioners, elected in 1868, was composed entirely of Republicans and included one black man, Robert Gwynn. Two years later the Democrats gained control of the board, and more than a century elapsed before another black man—Clarence E. Tucker, elected in 1978—served as a member of that body.

During Reconstruction the Republicans failed to win the county's vote in presidential elections, and only in the 1868 gubernatorial election did the county electorate deviate from its traditional Democratic stance and give a majority to Republican William W. Holden. (The only other example of a significant defection from the Democratic party occurred in 1838 when voters in Rockingham County awarded a thirty-one-vote majority to Whig Edward B. Dudley in the gubernatorial election of that year.)

The county's most important public figure of this era was Thomas Settle, Jr., a founder of the state Republican party. Prior to the Civil War, Settle, a wealthy planter and former Whig leader, had followed his cousin, David S. Reid, into the Democratic party. After the war Settle

Thomas Settle, Jr. (1831-1888), a founder of the state Republican party, was the county's leading public figure of the Reconstruction era. Photograph from *Green Bag*, IV (December, 1892), p. 570.

won election as a Republican to the state Senate, where he served as Speaker, and to the state supreme court. In 1871 he was appointed United States minister to Peru but resigned after a year because of poor health. He presided at the Republican National Convention of 1872 and was later defeated in a campaign for a seat in the United States Congress. His unsuccessful gubernatorial campaign in 1876 against Zebulon B. Vance, the "Battle of the Giants," is remembered as one of the most exciting and colorful campaigns in the state's history. Settle spent his last years in Florida, where he served as a federal district judge.

Although Ku Klux Klan violence was not as severe in Rockingham as in the neighboring counties of Caswell and Alamance, the county experienced a terror campaign in 1868-1869. Incidents reported in the Raleigh *North Carolina Standard* in August, 1869, involved the shooting of young Mary Lomax and the beating and abuse of black men and women. Superior Court Judge Albion Tourgée of Greensboro convened a special term of court in the county to hear a case brought against twenty alleged Klansmen, but the jury returned verdicts of not guilty. Klan offenses became so blatant that in 1870 the highly respected former governor Reid joined his cousin, Thomas Settle, in denouncing the Klan activity. Reid's public statements coincided with a statewide federal investigation of the Klan, which soon forced the secret organization to cease its activities in the state.

Postwar Agriculture

Tobacco remained the county's preeminent agricultural staple, rising in production from 4 million pounds in 1880 to over 9 million pounds by the end of the century. Demand for tobacco products had been strong during the Civil War and did not slacken in the postwar years. The principal type of tobacco grown during this period was the flue-cured brightleaf variety, which had been developed in Caswell County during the 1850s. John Marion Gallaway of Madison, the "biggest grower of flue-cured tobacco in the world," once owned 15,000 acres of tobacco in several counties and employed 300 tenant farmers to cultivate it. The county's other major crops were corn, oats, wheat, and hay. By the end of the century the county had 30,000 acres in corn, 18,000 acres in wheat, 17,000 acres in tobacco, 5,000 acres in oats, and 5,000 acres in hay.

VI. THE NEW SOUTH

Population Growth

In 1870 the county's population was down slightly (for the first and only time) to 15,708, having been 16,746 in 1860; but by 1900 it had more than doubled to 33,163. During this thirty-year period the first significant urban development began. The new towns of Price and Ruffin came into existence in 1868 and 1887 respectively, and the older communities were formally incorporated by the General Assembly: Reidsville in 1873, Leaksville in 1874, Madison in 1876, and Stoneville in 1887. Each of these towns experienced considerable growth. Reidsville, through the stimulus provided by the railroad, the growth of tobacco manufacturing, and the development of a tobacco market, mushroomed from a few families in 1865 to nearly 3,500 people in 1884. Leaksville's population remained stable at less than 300 until the railroad arrived in December, 1883, and then nearly tripled within a few years. Wentworth, although it boasted a gristmill and several tobacco factories, served primarily as the county's governmental center; its population remained stable at fewer than 500 people.

Most of the county's residents were farmers or farm laborers in 1870. Tobacco factories, which were farm based and were located throughout the county, hired males and females of both races, but the Morehead textile mill hired only white workers. Common occupations among blacks were carpenter and blacksmith, but blacks also followed the trades of painter, nurse, wagoner, plasterer, and boatman. By 1880 many additional occupations were open to blacks, some of whom had become merchants.

Reidsville and Tobacco Manufacturing

Reidsville at the close of the Civil War was so small that one traveler, John Richard Dennett, rode through and beyond the village in September, 1865, before realizing that he had missed it. Turning back on the road, Dennett found only a small railroad way station, a few houses, and one store. To Dennett, the Rockingham countryside was "the poorest I have yet seen, with crops that seem less abundant and healthy than those further north. . . ." He noted that there were few large plantations and was told by local inhabitants that Rockingham and Caswell counties were populated by "them triflin' people." In the area between Reidsville and Danville, Dennett observed mostly cornfields, although a few acres of tobacco apparently were visible also.

During the post-Civil War period the county's farm factories of the antebellum era were relocated in closer proximity to Reidsville in order to take advantage of the greatly expanded commercial opportunities afforded by the railroad that extended through the town. A market for the sale of tobacco soon evolved. Another common tobacco-related enterprise of the postwar period was the prizery, where bulk tobacco was crated or prized into large wooden hogsheads for shipment to markets. Just five years after his 1865 visit John Richard Dennett would have found in Reidsville a number of tobacco factories, a hotel, several merchants, shoemakers, wheelwrights, a harness maker, schoolteachers, and three physicians. Major Mortimer Oaks presided over the transformation of the town; he arrived in 1866 and opened the Piedmont Hotel and, soon afterward, a store. Prior to 1871 Oaks formed a partnership with James Dalton and began the manufacture of plug

Major Mortimer Oaks (left) came to Reidsville in 1866 and opened the Piedmont Hotel (right). His subsequent activities helped to transform the town from a sleepy village into a thriving industrial center. Photograph at left from Richard A. Saunders, Sr. (comp.), *Open Doors and Closed Windows of the First Baptist Church of Reidsville, North Carolina* (Reidsville: First Baptist Church, 1948), p. 258; at right from *Reidsville Review*, September 3, 1919.

tobacco. The following year Oaks and James Allen established the Piedmont Warehouse for the sale of tobacco, thus forming the basis of the town's modern tobacco industry.

In 1872 Reidsville's business and industry consisted of the Piedmont Warehouse, the Farmer's Warehouse, and several independent dealers. The town boasted a number of merchants, two hotels, a photographer, a cabinet shop, a Masonic lodge, two schools, and ten prizeries—one of which was owned by W. W. Davis, a black man. Well-known tobacco manufacturers in Reidsville during the late nineteenth century were Robert Harris, A. H. Motley, and John and E. M. Redd.

F. R. Penn of Patrick County, Virginia, moved to Reidsville in 1874 and with his brother S. C. Penn established the F. R. Penn Tobacco Company for the purpose of manufacturing both chewing and smoking tobacco. Popular plug brands produced by the Penns were Penn's

The Reidsville firm of A. H. Motley & Company was a well-known tobacco-manufacturing concern during the late nineteenth century. The company billed itself as "the largest plug tobacco works in the state." Engraving from *Weekly Review* (Reidsville), February 27, 1889.

Natural Leaf and Penn's Red J, and their leading smoking tobacco brands were Gold Crumbs and Queen Quality.

In 1877 Robert P. Richardson, Jr. (1855-1922), established a tobacco factory that launched a new smoking tobacco known as Old North State; this product became a leading regional brand. Richardson's success influenced other local manufacturers (who primarily were producing chewing tobacco) to make smoking tobacco, and by 1900 Reidsville was second only to Durham in total production of this article.

In 1890 Reidsville boasted eight plug factories and three smoking-tobacco factories that together employed 1,800 people and processed over 4 million pounds of tobacco. Other local industries consisted of a cotton mill, a box factory, 2 grist- and sawmills, 3 carriage-repair shops, a paper box factory, 2 harness makers, a granite works, 3 brickyards, and a bucket factory. Reidsville was incorporated in 1873 with Mortimer Oaks as the first mayor. Another important citizen in the town's development during this period was attorney Andrew J. Boyd, who organized the Bank of Reidsville in 1882 and became its first president. (The town's second such institution was the Citizens Bank, founded in 1885.) In 1889 Boyd established the Reidsville Cotton Mill and likewise served as its first president.

By 1885 Leaksville had also become a tobacco market, and several tobacco-manufacturing firms had located in the community. There were eight plug factories in the town in 1893. Doctor Franklin King (1843-1922) came to Leaksville from Henry County, Virginia, during the 1880s. He was initially engaged in buying and selling leaf tobacco and then in tobacco manufacturing. Over the years he accumulated a considerable amount of property. In 1889 he and W. R. Walker founded the Bank of

Leaksville, the town's first locally owned bank. King served as president of the bank until the year of his death, at which time the bank was reorganized as the Leaksville Bank and Trust Company. An ardent Baptist, King was a founder and trustee of the Leaksville-Spray Institute and a deacon, association moderator, and benefactor of Leaksville's King Memorial Baptist Church. His Victorian Norman mansion, erected on Bridge Street in 1874, is the outstanding nineteenth-century residence in the community.

Improvements to the Dan River

In 1878 the federal government authorized a survey of the Dan River from Clarksville, Virginia, to Danbury, North Carolina. A government engineer conducted the survey and submitted detailed reports in 1879 and 1880. As a result, the federal government appropriated $22,500 for improvements to shallow-draft steam navigation on the river between Danville and Madison. Erected at various points along the river were rock wing dams and sluices, some of which have remained intact until the present time in spite of the fact that they have had no maintenance for a century. James Turner Morehead of Leaksville, who had secured the steam navigation rights to the river, was the catalyst for the survey and resulting improvements. Bateau traffic continued on the Dan into the 1880s, but the coming of the railroad to Leaksville in 1883 and Madison in 1889 provided a faster and better form of transportation. Private excursions on the river persisted well into the twentieth century, although commercial traffic probably ended about 1890.

Railroad Development

As elsewhere, railroad construction expanded considerably in Rockingham County during the postwar era. The Dan River provided Leaksville with a minimal link to the outside world, but community leaders realized that only a railroad could provide adequate access to a wider market area. In 1879, under an act of the General Assembly, Leaksville Township voted to issue bonds to finance the purchase of stock in any railroad that would lay tracks through the township. During this period the General Assembly chartered several railroad companies that proposed a connection to the county: the Dan River & Yadkin, the Winston-Salem & Madison, the Danville, Mocksville & Southwestern, and the Danville & New River. In 1880 several of these companies consolidated to become the North Carolina Midland Railroad, which proposed a new rail route from Virginia through Leaksville, Madison, and Winston to Mooresville. James Turner Morehead was named vice-president of the new company. The North Carolina Midland road secured a right-of-way in the Dan valley and engaged in some culvert construction and grading, but the proposed line through

Rockingham County was never built. Meanwhile, construction of the Danville, Mocksville & Southwestern road was begun from Leaksville Junction, and on December 21, 1883, this narrow-gauge line was completed between Danville and Leaksville. The first locomotive to arrive in Leaksville was named the "Lily C. Morehead." By 1889 the Danville, Mocksville & Southwestern road had been merged into the Danville & Western Railroad Company.

James T. Morehead was a director of the Western Railroad Company, which in 1879 became the Cape Fear & Yadkin Valley Railway Company. This line connected Wilmington and Mount Airy. By the summer of 1889 a branch line of the Cape Fear & Yadkin Valley road was in operation from Stokesdale in northwestern Guilford County to Madison. This railroad was eventually purchased by the Southern Railway System and was operated as the Atlantic & Yadkin Railroad.

Both Leaksville and Madison townships owned stock in the North Carolina Midland Railroad. The Southern Railway System eventually absorbed the Midland road and continued to pay a 3 percent dividend on the Midland shares held by the townships. Since 1907 the trustees of Leaksville Township's dividend fund have dispensed nearly $50,000 for various public construction projects in the township. Revenues were used to pave the road between Leaksville and Spray in 1907; to erect seven school buildings in the township; and for construction of a public library in 1936, an armory in 1938, the recorder's court building in 1941, and Morehead Stadium in 1952. More recently, funds have been given to Tri-City Hospital, Morehead Memorial Hospital, the Eden Public Library, and the Eden YMCA. The railroad stock owned by Madison Township was sold in 1981, with the proceeds used for the preservation of the Scales Law Office.

Little is known about the Rockingham & Caswell Railroad, which was incorporated in 1907, but a recently discovered map of the proposed rail line indicates that it was projected to connect Yanceyville with all of the major towns in Rockingham County. Although survey and planning work was conducted for several months, the road was never built.

James Turner Morehead and the New South

Upon the death of his father in 1866, James Turner Morehead moved from Greensboro to Leaksville to direct the family enterprises. An apostle of industrial development, Morehead expanded the mills, established the forerunner of the Spray Water Power and Land Company, promoted railroads, and supported industrial research. The Leaksville Factory complex on the Smith River then consisted of a cotton mill, a woolen mill, the company store (Spray Mercantile Company), and company housing for the workers and managers. During this period the name Spray began to be used for the industrial complex and was formally incorporated into the Spray Water Power and Land Company in 1889. Various members of the Morehead family were involved in managing the extensive family businesses. Noah Ford, brother-in-law of James T. Morehead, supervised the wool blanket mill, which in 1884 won a gold medal at the State Exposition in Raleigh. B. Frank Mebane, Morehead's son-in-law, and W. R. Walker, a cousin, were the principal officers of Spray Water Power and Land Company. Improvements were made to the original dam and canal, including the digging of a parallel canal, in order to increase the availability of waterpower. A state geological survey made in 1899 found that the canal developed a total of 600 horsepower. At that time the waterway was the source of power for Leaksville Cotton Mill (with 400 looms), a flour and gristmill, Spray Cotton Mill (with 12,064 spindles), Leaksville Woolen Mill, and Nantucket Mill (with 400 looms).

Letterhead of Spray Water Power and Land Company, ca. 1900. Photograph supplied by the author.

By 1892 James T. Morehead had become involved in an attempt to develop an economical process for making aluminum. With Thomas L. Willson, a Canadian chemist, he formed in 1891 a partnership known as the Willson Aluminum Company. Willson hoped to extract aluminum by combining aluminum oxide and carbon at a high temperature. Beside the canal at the present site of Spray Cotton Mill, Willson constructed an electric-arc furnace, which was powered by electricity generated by the waterway. This is believed to have been the first such furnace in the United States. One frustrating failure led to another, but on May 2, 1892, when the furnace was scraped out, the waste—which included aluminum oxide, carbon, lime, and tar—was dunked in a cooling vat, where it fizzled and emitted a gas. Morehead's son, John Motley Morehead III, a recent chemistry graduate of the University of North Carolina, identified the solid waste as a new chemical compound, calcium carbide. The younger Morehead did not have gas-analysis apparatus, so he dispatched a sample of the gaseous material to the university at Chapel Hill, where Professor Francis P. Venable and a student assistant, William Rand Kenan, identified the gas as acetylene.

James T. Morehead did not immediately find a practical use for his discoveries, and the Panic of 1893 bankrupted him. He left Spray for New York City to seek northern capital and in 1894 founded the Electro-Gas Company for the purpose of manufacturing and selling carbide and acetylene. Further experimentation led to the discovery of ferrochromium and ferrosilicon alloys, which were later used in the processing of steel for armor plate. During the 1890s the United States Navy was busily engaged in acquiring new steam-powered, armor-plated naval vessels. This program of naval expansion and particularly the outbreak of the Spanish-American War brought Morehead renewed prosperity and financial security. He later developed power sites on the James River in Virginia and on the Kanawha River in West Virginia. His patents on chemical processes and metal alloys and his industrial developments in Virginia and West Virginia led after his death to the formation of Union Carbide Corporation, one of the world's largest industrial entities.

James Turner Morehead (1840-1908) was a leader in the industrialization of Rockingham County during the post-Civil War period. This portrait of Morehead in the uniform of a Confederate officer, an oil on canvas rendered by Adrian Lamb, presently hangs in the Morehead Planetarium at Chapel Hill. Photograph from copy in North Carolina Collection.

Through benefactions made by James Turner Morehead's son, John Motley Morehead III of Rye, New York, some of the wealth earned by Union Carbide came back to James T. Morehead's native state and county. The philanthropic gifts made by John Motley Morehead III to the University of North Carolina in the form of the Morehead Scholarships, the Morehead-Patterson Bell Tower, and the Morehead Planetarium are well known, but outside of Rockingham County little is known of his gifts to his hometown: a stadium and chimes to the high school that bears his name and a major contribution toward the construction of Morehead Memorial Hospital, a modern health care facility.

Enoch W. Moore: Inventor

Enoch W. Moore (1868-1952) grew up on Belews Creek, where his father, James W. Moore, operated a gristmill, a sawmill, a machine shop, a foundry, and a smithy. Possessing a native scientific mind, young Enoch Moore as a student at Trinity College excelled in physics and in the practical application of electricity. During a summer vacation he built a dynamo and attached it to the waterwheel of his father's mill. He then installed an electric lighting system in the mill; this was the first commercial use of electricity in Rockingham County. Moore later built the first electric plant in Reidsville for the Southern Electric Light and Construction Company and constructed similar plants throughout the Southeast. He established the Moore-Edenfield Electric Manufacturing Company and about 1900 settled in Pittsburgh, Pennsylvania, where in 1916 he founded Mooreco Enterprises, which developed electric furnaces, dryers, and an electric vacuum cleaner. Moore eventually held 130 United States patents.

The Development of the Mayo Valley

The western portion of Rockingham County slumbered until an energetic entrepreneur of the New South, Francis Henry Fries of Salem, recognized the Mayo valley as a potentially valuable center for industrial development. Fries, the son of a Moravian textile manufacturer, had a remarkable business career as a railroad builder, textile manufacturer, builder of the first hydroelectric power plant in the state, and founder of Wachovia Bank and Trust Company. Businessmen of Winston and Salem were concerned that their towns, which during the post-Civil War period had been connected only by a spur to the important North Carolina Railroad at Greensboro, would not grow and prosper; therefore, they sought to have a railroad constructed from Salem to Roanoke and from Roanoke to the Midwest. The Roanoke & Salem Railway was chartered in 1887, and young Francis Fries was put in charge of construction of rights-of-way. Fries projected a route through the Mayo valley and envisioned various potential industrial sites. Construction of the Roanoke & Salem's southern section, which linked Salem and Martinsville, Virginia, was completed by April, 1891, and by the end of that year the last rail had been laid on the line from Martinsville to Roanoke. The following year the Roanoke & Salem Railway Company was sold to the Norfolk & Western Railway System, which operates the line at the present time. The railroad brought industry to the Mayo Valley, and the new towns of Avalon and Mayodan soon sprang to life. The railroad also served to rejuvenate the older towns of Stoneville, Madison, and Price.

Stoneville, founded prior to the Civil War near Mayo post office, had been a crossroads where Francis J. and Pinckney Stone maintained stores. At this location in 1875 Robert H. Lewis began the manufacture of a brand of plug tobacco known as Carolina Morning and the same year opened Farmer's Warehouse and founded the local tobacco market.

With the Roanoke & Salem Railway came a hotel, and trains frequently stopped in Stoneville, where passengers could obtain a midday meal. The railroad brought steady growth to the town. The Stoneville Depot (1891), no longer in service, is the oldest extant railroad building in the county. Early in the twentieth century there were two newspapers in Stoneville: the *News*, founded in 1911, and the *Observer*, established in 1914.

The falls of the Mayo at the Cedar Point Mountain water gap offered an excellent site for a mill, and in 1892 Francis Fries persuaded other capitalists, including William C. Ruffin of Rocky Mount and Washington Duke of Durham, to invest in an enterprise that became known as Mayo Mills. Following the construction of a dam and canal, a yarn-producing mill began operations in the spring of 1896 with Fries as president and Ruffin as secretary and treasurer. The Piedmont Land Company developed an adjoining mill village. A small hamlet soon sprang up in the vicinity of the mill; it was named Mayodan and was incorporated in 1899 with W. C. Ruffin as the first mayor. By 1900 the population of Mayodan was 904. Mayo Mills became part of Washington Mills Corporation in 1921.

Two miles north of the Mayo Mills, Fries and Ruffin selected another site at which the flow of the Mayo River appeared to be strong enough to generate power. They named the site Avalon and in 1899 erected a four-story brick mill there. The mill was powered by two waterwheels that together generated 1,200 horsepower. A village soon evolved at the mill site, attracting merchants, and within a few years about sixty houses had been erected. Disaster struck the town on June 15, 1911, however, when the mill was totally destroyed by fire. The company did not rebuild the facility, but the following year it expanded the Mayo Mills at Mayodan, where many former Avalon workers found work. The company moved the Avalon houses to Mayodan by rolling some of them on logs pulled by large teams of horses. Over a two-year period the town was literally moved away. The remaining waterwheels were converted to the production of electricity and until 1968 generated power for the Washington Mills plant in Mayodan.

With the railroad providing the principal stimulus for development, Madison grew into a busy town by the end of the nineteenth century. In 1898 tobacco was the dominant factor in the economy. The town then boasted 3 leaf houses, 2 tobacco warehouses, the Penn brothers' tobacco factory (which manufactured plug tobacco), 2 hotels, 8 general merchants, 2 cabinetmakers, a newspaper, several livery stables, a hardware store, a blacksmith, an icehouse, a furniture store, a harness and jewelry store, a grocery, and a restaurant. The Bank of Madison was founded in 1899 with John M. Galloway as president. Black residents of Madison established barbershops and restaurants in the town by the turn of the century. A telephone exchange with twenty subscribers existed by 1905.

Mayo Mills (top) began operations in 1896 at the falls of the Mayo River. Three years later the new village of Mayodan (center) was incorporated. Near the turn of the century the village of Avalon evolved at the site of a mill near a dam and canal on the Mayo River (bottom). Photograph at top from picture postcard, ca. 1910, in the files of the Division of Archives and History; at center (ca. 1917) courtesy Jeff Bullins, Mayodan; at bottom courtesy Special Collections, Rockingham Community College Library.

Late Nineteenth-Century Politics

Rockingham County's traditional ties to the Democratic party were broken during the 1890s when the Populist party became a major factor in the 1892 election. Although Democrat Elias Carr won the gubernatorial election, he and Republican David M. Furches each received 1,881 votes in Rockingham County, while the Populist candidate, Wyatt P. Exum, polled 905 votes and the candidate of the Prohibition party received 15 votes. The 1892 presidential election was the first instance in the county's history in which a Democratic candidate failed to receive a majority of the ballots cast: Republican Benjamin Harrison carried the county over Democrat Grover Cleveland by a vote of 1,961 to 1,784—a margin of 177 votes. The Populist presidential candidate, James B. Weaver, who received 853 votes in the county, clearly drew his strength from disaffected Democrats. In 1896 William McKinley, the victorious Republican candidate for president, carried the county over Democrat William Jennings Bryan by a narrow margin.

Alfred M. Scales, Democrat and former Confederate brigadier general, represented the county's congressional district in the United States House of Representatives from 1875 to 1884; he resigned following his election as governor of North Carolina. His congressional seat was then won by Democrat James Wesley Reid (1849-1902), a Wentworth attorney who was known in his day as "the silver-tongued orator." Reid managed the Wright Tavern with his aunt, Nannie Wright, and during this period the establishment became known as the Reid Hotel. In 1887 Reid moved to Idaho, where he remained active in public affairs. Thomas Settle III (1865-1919), Wentworth attorney and Republican, served the district as a United States representative from 1893 to 1897 and was an unsuccessful candidate for governor in 1912.

Serving as state senators from Rockingham County during the late nineteenth century were W. N. Mebane of Madison (who was also a superior court judge), James Turner Morehead, and Hugh Reid Scott. Elected to the state House of Representatives were Dr. A. B. Johns, David Settle, W. N. Mebane, James Dodge Glenn, Pryor Reynolds, John M. Galloway, and John R. Webster (who in 1887 was Speaker of the House). John Henry Dillard served as a member of the state supreme court from 1879 to 1881.

Education in the Late Nineteenth Century

The post-Civil War era was one of growth for education. The state system of common schools for whites deteriorated during the early Reconstruction period, but in 1869 the legislature authorized creation of a new system of racially segregated public schools; this system operated with limited success during the ensuing decade. Private schools remained an important factor in elementary and secondary education until the twentieth century.

In Reidsville Mollie Irvin and Sallie Brent conducted a school for girls. F. P. Hobgood opened an academy for boys and girls in 1870, and two years later the Reidsville Seminary for girls was organized with Emma Scales and Annie Hughes as the teachers. The Reidsville Male Academy, under the direction of George R. McNeill and C. R. Owen, operated during the 1880s.

Academies dominated private education in Madison. Dr. Lewis H. Shook continued to operate Beulah Academy, then open to boys and girls, until 1872. He was followed as superintendent by Rufus Smith (1872-1880), Hazel Norwood (1882-1885), J. L. Holmes (1886-1891), and in 1891 by the Reverend Andrew C. Betts, who also founded the first public library in Madison. The first educational institution for blacks in Madison was a subscription school that opened in 1880 with a three-month school term. Milton Stamps, a white man, was the first teacher. John Martin, a student at this school, became a leader in the development of black education.

Leaksville Academy reopened after the war with John R. Winston as the teacher. Winston's two most prominent students were future governor Robert B. Glenn and future lieutenant governor Charles A. Reynolds. By 1875 Nathaniel W. Smith was conducting a school in Leaksville for boys and girls; he was assisted by Nannie Hayden. The Leaksville Practical High School opened in 1886 with B. W. Ray and Helen Betts as the teachers. This school offered a curriculum of music, three levels of English instruction, bookkeeping, and Latin for a tuition of $10.00 to $20.00 per term.

Other private schools in the county during this period were the Reidsville Female Seminary, directed by Mattie Mebane and Bettie Hall, and the Wentworth Male Academy, which had been revived by D. M. Weatherly; both of these institutions were located in the vicinity of Wentworth. W. B. Harris opened the Stoneville Academy in 1885. In 1887 R. S. Powell was conducting a coeducational school at Mt. Hermon Church.

Records of the public school system indicate that 37 school districts with school committees existed in Rockingham County in 1877. At that time there were 33 public schools and 5 private academies for whites and 9 public schools and 10 private schools for blacks. A total of 4,155 white children and 2,540 black children attended these schools, with the black institutions receiving proportionately more money. Teachers earned an average salary of about $50.00 per year.

A new era in public education began on March 10, 1881, with the election of N. S. Smith as county superintendent of public instruction. In 1881 there were 6,897 students and 95 teachers in the Rockingham County schools. Only the first three grades were offered, and the school term was about thirteen and one half weeks long. The following year, when the county board of education balked at supporting teachers' institutes (for in-service training) and paying adequate salaries, the teachers held protest meetings. Superintendent Smith resigned in support of the teachers but was reinstated within a year by order of the state attorney general. Appropriations gradually increased, and Smith was able to implement teachers' institutes for both white and black teachers.

In 1887 George R. McNeill was named superintendent of Reidsville's graded schools, and a new public system was begun. The principal of Reidsville's school for whites was C. R. Owen, and J. E. Dellinger headed the school for blacks. The earliest known county school for blacks was in Madison and was taught by Jane Richardson in 1870. The school operated in a building on Idol Street until 1902, when John Martin and others purchased a former tobacco warehouse and converted it for use as a new school.

Churches in the Late Nineteenth Century

Some of the leading churches in the county at the present time were founded during the late nineteenth century. The Reverend Jacob Doll organized Reidsville's First Presbyterian Church in 1875; the Reverend David I. Craig was one of its noted ministers. The First Baptist Church in Reidsville was established in 1869 when the Hogan's Creek Baptist congregation was persuaded to move to a site that had been donated by William Lindsey; P. H. Fontaine was named pastor the following year. In 1885 the Baptist State Convention assembled in Reidsville. The Main Street Methodist Church was organized in the home of William Lindsey, and by 1878 a building had been completed. The congregation consisted initially of eighteen members and was headed by the Reverend Caiphias Norman. The present building, a striking brick Romanesque structure, was completed in 1891. Saint Thomas Episcopal Church was founded in 1883, and within two years a frame building had been erected. Because of encroachment by industry, church members sold this building to the Zion Baptist Church, a black congregation, about 1900. The present Saint Thomas Church building was constructed before 1915.

During the antebellum period Rockingham County slaves were regarded as members of their masters' churches. For a brief time after the war freedmen continued to attend the predominantly white churches, but they soon began to organize their own Sunday schools and congregations. By 1874 the Reverend Samuel Jones had founded a black Baptist church in Reidsville, and J. McGehee, a black member of Reidsville's First Baptist Church, had withdrawn in order to join Jones's congregation. Saint Paul Methodist Church, a black congregation, was established by 1890 with the Reverend J. D. Hairston as pastor.

In Leaksville, which had not experienced the degree of growth enjoyed by Reidsville, few new churches were organized; however, several of the antebellum congregations occupied new buildings. The congregation of the First Baptist Church erected a new brick building, its present sanctuary, in 1884-1885. In 1886 Rawleigh Dillard, a black barber, established a Sunday school for members of his race. From this beginning came the Saint John Methodist Church, erected two years later under the leadership of the Reverend Marcus Mundy. Another black congregation organized in Leaksville during this period was Mt. Sinai Baptist.

In Madison during the 1880s there was an interdenominational black church from which the Reverend M. J. Bullock formed Saint Stephens Methodist, which occupied a building by 1890. The Beulah Baptist Church was founded in 1890 with the Reverend J. P. Alexander as pastor. James E. Foust, a deacon of Saint Stephens, began holding services in his home in 1901 and eventually built Mount Carmel Holiness Tabernacle.

Several churches were organized in Mayodan toward the end of the century. Under the lay leadership of Howard E. Rondthaler and Samuel P. Tesh, a Moravian congregation was formed and a church building erected in 1896. This church, the first in the community, also housed the town's first school and public library. The Avalon Moravian Church was a mission of the Mayodan congregation. In 1897 the Episcopal Church of the Messiah was founded by the Reverend James H. Williams. There were several Episcopal missions in the western section of the county during the early twentieth century, but only the Church of the Messiah has endured to the present time. Mayodan's Baptists organized in 1901, and the following year Methodist and Pentecostal Holiness congregations were founded.

Ruffin Methodist Church, founded in 1874 with the Reverend William C. Norman as pastor, was the first church in that community. Oscar P. Fitzgerald (1829-1911), a Methodist bishop, grew up in the Ruffin community. In 1855 he went to California, where he was a Methodist preacher and editor of the *Pacific Methodist Advocate*. In 1878 he became editor of the *Christian Advocate*, published in Nashville, Tennessee. In 1890 he was elected a bishop. Over the years he published a number of books, including memoirs, sermons, and meditations.

VII. THE TWENTIETH CENTURY

Modern Population Trends

Rockingham County has enjoyed steady growth in the twentieth century. The population has more than doubled, rising from 33,163 in 1900 to 83,426 in 1980. Only three municipalities were incorporated during this period: Draper in 1949, Spray in 1951, and Eden, formed in 1967 from the consolidation of Leaksville, Spray, Draper, and a central area that separated the three towns. With its formation Eden became the largest city in the county, and the merger has proven to be a resounding success.

By 1970 nearly half of the county's total population was classified as urban. The county's five largest municipalities in 1980 were: Eden (15,672 people), Reidsville (12,492), Madison (2,806), Mayodan (2,627), and Stoneville (1,054). The nonwhite population has remained fairly constant at about 20 percent. The only significant change in the ethnic composition of the county's population has come from an increasing influx of Mexican-Americans. Wentworth has experienced a sharp population decline and is presently the smallest county seat in the state. Because of its central location, however, several county institutions have located there—Rockingham Community College, the county mental health center, and most recently a consolidated armory for the county's National Guard units.

Draper

Draper was conceived in 1905 as a model village by the German-American Corporation, a textile firm, and named for William F. Draper, a company executive. In 1911 Marshall Field and Company, a large Chicago corporation, acquired a textile mill that had opened in Draper in 1906. The Rockingham Land Company developed the town. Beginning with W. T. Coleman, merchants came to the village, churches were organized, a railroad depot was built in 1907, a school was opened in 1908, and the Bank of Draper was established in 1920.

Draper was incorporated in 1949, and Archie S. Daniels, who later served as the first county manager, became the town's first mayor. The first police chief was Carl H. Axsom, who was later elected county sheriff. Axsom was sheriff longer than anyone else in the county's history, and during his tenure he directed the transition of the department into a modern law enforcement agency. Another local political leader from Draper, Mrs. Virginia Tiller, was the first woman in the county's history to be elected a county commissioner.

Three twentieth-century views of towns in Rockingham County. TOP: Wentworth, ca. 1910, with county courthouse at right; CENTER: bird's-eye view of the business section of Reidsville, ca. 1924; BOTTOM: Washington Street in downtown Leaksville, ca. 1950. Photograph at top courtesy Miss Mary Baker, Reidsville; at center from Albert Y. Drummond (ed.), *Drummond's Pictorial Atlas of North Carolina* (Charlotte: Albert Y. Drummond, 1924), p. 104; at bottom from *State*, XIX (August 25, 1951), p. 6.

Eden

By the 1960s the Tri-Cities—Leaksville, Spray, and Draper, each with a sizable population—had grown together physically. In 1960 the population of Leaksville was 6,458; Spray, 4,544; and Draper, 3,322. Earlier attempts to merge the three towns had failed, but during the 1960s the unincorporated central area that separated the three towns became the site of residential development, a shopping center, and the modern general office of Fieldcrest Mills. The initial step toward consolidation was the formation in 1963 of the Eden Metropolitan Sewerage District. Voters had defeated referendums on the question of merger in 1959 and 1963, but in 1967 the local chamber of commerce and the Jaycees began actively promoting the proposition. A new referendum was approved in all three towns, and the electorate selected Eden, from William Byrd's "Land of Eden," as the name for the new city. G. W. Armfield was named mayor of a temporary governing board, and Jones Norman became mayor of the first permanent city council.

Twentieth-Century Politics

The Democratic party retained its dominant position in county politics, although five times in this century a non-Democrat carried the vote of the county in presidential elections: Republicans William Howard Taft in 1908 (by 21 votes), Herbert Hoover in 1928, Dwight D. Eisenhower in 1956 (by 95 votes), and Richard Nixon in 1972, and American party candidate George C. Wallace in 1968. Wallace is the only third-party presidential candidate in the county's history to poll more than a token vote. In 1928 unsuccessful Republican gubernatorial candidate H. F. Seawell outpolled Democrat O. Max Gardner in the county by 46 votes, and in 1972 the first Republican governor of North Carolina elected in the twentieth century, James E. Holshouser, Jr., carried the county. In all other elections on the state and national levels, Democratic candidates have usually won significant victories.

The only United States congressman from Rockingham County elected in this century was textile executive John Motley Morehead II (1866-1923), who was a native of Charlotte but resided in Spray and worked for the various family enterprises. Morehead, a Republican, served in Congress from 1909 to 1911 and later became chairman of the State Republican Executive Committee and also served on the party's national committee.

The county has been ably represented in the General Assembly during the twentieth century. Among the county's state senators have been Reuben D. Reid, Allan D. Ivie, Allen H. Gwyn, J. Hampton Price, T. Clarence Stone, Jule McMichael, Frank R. Penn, Wesley D. Webster, and Conrad Duncan. In 1943 Price was president pro tempore of the Senate. Stone, a former mayor of Stoneville, was president pro tempore of the Senate in 1963.

74

Members of the state House of Representatives were T. Clarence Stone (1935-1947), Joe W. Garrett (1936-1941), Radford G. Powell (1949-1959), Earl W. Vaughn (1961-1969), and Jule McMichael (1967-1971). Senators Conrad Duncan and Wesley Webster also served terms in the House. In 1969 Earl W. Vaughn of Eden became the first Speaker of the House from Rockingham County since 1887. Later that year Vaughn was appointed to the state court of appeals, where he continues to serve. In 1931 Mrs. Lily Morehead Mebane of Spray, who had been decorated by the king of Serbia for her war-relief work, became the first and only woman from the county to serve in the state House of Representatives.

The county's leading jurist of the twentieth century has been Miss Susie Marshall Sharp of Reidsville. A 1928 graduate of the University of North Carolina Law School, Miss Sharp began a practice in her hometown with her father, J. M. Sharp. In 1949 she became the first woman in the state to serve as a superior court judge, and in 1962 she

Susie Marshall Sharp of Reidsville became the state's first female superior court judge in 1949 and later served as an associate justice of the North Carolina Supreme Court from 1962 to 1974 and as chief justice from 1974 to 1979. Photograph (1949) from David Leroy Corbitt (ed.), *Public Addresses, Letters, and Papers of William Kerr Scott, Governor of North Carolina, 1949-1953* (Raleigh: State of North Carolina, 1957), facing p. 95.

became a member of the North Carolina Supreme Court. She was elected chief justice of the state supreme court in 1974 and retained that position until her retirement in 1979. In 1976 *Time* magazine selected her as one of a dozen American "Women of the Year." Other well-known judges were Henry P. Lane of Leaksville, who served on the superior court from 1910 to 1926, and Allen H. Gwyn, who was a superior-court judge from 1939 to 1969. Through his "Work, Earn, Save" program, the innovative Judge Gwyn sought to rehabilitate criminals—particularly first offenders—and break the frequently repeated cycle of return to prison.

Two natives of the county, Robert Brodnax Glenn of Winston-Salem and Capus M. Waynick of High Point, have served their state and nation well. Glenn was governor of North Carolina from 1905 to 1909; Waynick, a former newspaper editor, was adjutant-general of the state and served as United States ambassador to Nicaragua (1949-1951) and Colombia (1951-1953).

Luther Hartwell Hodges was the outstanding public figure from the county in this century. Hodges was an industrialist, governor of North Carolina from 1954 to 1961, and United States secretary of commerce from 1961 to 1964. He served his state well as governor by advocating moderation during the initial period of public school desegregation and by consistently encouraging industries to locate in the state. In addition, Hodges was instrumental in developing the industrial education centers that were the forerunners of the state community college system and in creating the Research Triangle Park—possibly the most significant step ever taken for the state's economic future. A native of Pittsylvania County, Virginia, Hodges was born in 1898 in a log tenant house, but his

In this cartoon by Bill Sanders an impatient Governor Luther Hodges awaits notification by President-elect John F. Kennedy that he is to be nominated for the cabinet post of secretary of commerce. Cartoon from *Greensboro Daily News*, December 3, 1960; reproduced by permission.

father moved to Leaksville in 1901. After graduating from the University of North Carolina in 1919, Hodges joined Marshall Field and Company, where he became a production manager, general manager, and by 1945 a vice-president. He retired two years later but in 1950 went to West Germany as a textile consultant for the United States Economic Cooperation Administration. After returning home in 1952, he surprised everyone by running successfully for lieutenant governor of North Carolina. When Governor William B. Umstead died in November, 1954, Hodges succeeded him and in 1956 won reelection to a four-year term in his own right.

Toward a Modern Economy

For more than a century Rockingham County has possessed a broad economic base anchored equally on industry and agriculture. Tobacco production grew from more than 8 million pounds in 1909 to more than 9½ million pounds by 1924. Other important crops were corn, wheat, and hay, but as early as 1918 a study of the county's agriculture emphasized the fact that not enough livestock and food crops were being produced. The introduction of the county agent in 1909 and of the home demonstration program in 1919 led to greater diversification. Although 80 percent of the county's farm income at the present time is generated by tobacco, increasing amounts of beef, pork, corn and silage, wheat, hay, soybeans, broilers, hens, milk, vegetables, and fruits are going to market. A recent trend has been the expansion of pick-your-own vegetables and fruits (particularly strawberries) and an increase in the number of orchards.

The Tobacco Industry

Around the turn of the century American industrial growth centered on the formation of monopolies or trusts, which destroyed effective competition. The gigantic American Tobacco Trust formed by James Buchanan (Buck) Duke absorbed practically all of the small smoking-tobacco firms and most of the chewing-tobacco manufacturers of the time. American Tobacco purchased the Reidsville firm of F. R. Penn and Company in 1911, the same year in which a government antitrust suit forced a dissolution of the monopoly.

Charles A. Penn (1868-1931), an executive with the local company, became a director of the American Tobacco Company in 1913 and assistant production manager in New York. Interested in product research, Penn perfected the blend for a new cigarette known as Lucky Strike, which later became one of the all-time leading brands in the history of the industry. At Penn's suggestion, a factory to produce Lucky Strikes

The American Tobacco Company has long been one of Reidsville's industrial mainstays. Shown above are three of the company's factory buildings that comprise a portion of the American Tobacco complex in northern Reidsville. Photograph from Laura A. W. Phillips, *Reidsville, North Carolina: An Inventory of Historic & Architectural Resources* (Reidsville: North Carolina Department of Cultural Resources, Division of Archives and History, and Reidsville Historic Properties Commission, 1981), p. 37.

was built in Reidsville, and for many years the "Lucky City" was identified with the famous cigarette brand. Penn became American Tobacco Company's vice-president of manufacturing in 1916 and is credited with the idea for the Lucky Strike advertising slogan, "It's Toasted!" Although Penn worked in New York, he always regarded Reidsville as his home; and he contributed in many ways to the development of the community. He was a founder and a major benefactor of the Annie Penn Memorial Hospital, which has been expanded several times and provides excellent health care for the county. Following Penn's death in New York, his body was returned to Reidsville. Thousands of mourners attended his funeral, the largest ever held in the county. Largely because of Charlie Penn, American Tobacco (now a part of American Brands, Inc.) remains one of the three major industries in Rockingham County and the economic foundation of the city of Reidsville.

An industrial survey of the county conducted in 1918 enumerated the following tobacco-manufacturing firms, all of which were located in Reidsville: Robert Harris and Brother, the Penn Branch of American Tobacco Company, the Piedmont Cigar Company, and R. P. Richardson, Jr., and Company. R. P. Richardson continued to produce Old North State smoking tobacco until Brown and Williamson Tobacco Company purchased his factory in 1926. In Leaksville the J. B. Taylor Tobacco Company manufactured chewing tobacco during the 1890s.

The Textile Industry

Benjamin Franklin Mebane, a son-in-law of James Turner Morehead, became president of Spray Water Power and Land Company in 1892 and directed the operations of a family textile empire in the community until well into the twentieth century. Mebane was also president of the Leaksville Cotton and Woolen Mill Company. W. R. Walker, a cousin of James T. Morehead, was secretary and treasurer of the two companies. In 1893 the original yarn mill was destroyed by fire; Mebane had a new mill erected on the site and then embarked on a program of erecting a

Benjamin Franklin Mebane directed and expanded the Morehead family textile enterprises from 1892 until well into the twentieth century. Engraving from *Farmer and Mechanic* (Raleigh), October 24, 1905.

new textile facility almost every year. Another Mebane operation was the Spray Mercantile Company, a mill store founded in 1892 and eventually acquired by Rufus P. Ray. The mercantile building, the first part of which was built in 1904, is the most architecturally elaborate commercial building in the county.

The enterprising Mebane's next venture came in 1896 with the establishment of Spray Cotton Mill, a yarn operation. Mebane obtained additional capital for the cotton mill from Dr. Karl von Ruck of Asheville, who eventually obtained ownership of the facility. In 1914 von Ruck asked his nephew, Karl Bishopric of Canada, to come to Spray to oversee operation of the mill. At the present time Spray Cotton Mill is the oldest continuously operating textile plant in the county and is still family owned and managed by Karl Bishopric's son Welsford. It produces high-quality cotton yarn under the label Spray-Spun. The corporation also manufactures textured yarn at another plant.

The most intensive period of development associated with Frank Mebane came with the establishment of Nantucket Mill in 1898, American Warehouse in 1899, Lily Mill in 1900, Spray Woolen Mill and Morehead Cotton Mills in 1902, Rhode Island Mill in 1903, and German-American Mill in 1905. As a consequence of Mebane's ever-expanding vision, he greatly overextended his resources, and a 1911 business recession damaged him financially. For years Marshall Field and Company had invested in Mebane's schemes. When the mills went bankrupt Marshall Field, Mebane's leading creditor, took control of them. By maneuvering quickly, Mebane was able to retain his home, a good deal of land, Morehead Cotton Mills, and Leaksville Cotton Mill. Marshall Field soon established Thread Mills Company, which took control of Nantucket, Lily, Rhode Island, German-American, and Spray Woolen mills as well as American Warehouse. Products manufactured by the various mills at this time were yarns, ginghams, outings, and cotton and wool blankets. Thread Mills Company later became known as Carolina Cotton and Woolen Mills Company.

In 1953 Marshall Field and Company sold its mill holdings in the Tri-Cities area to Fieldcrest Mills, Inc. Since that time Fieldcrest has modernized the local mills and presently produces quality finished goods—blankets, electric blankets, sheets, towels, bedspreads, rugs, and the famous Karastan oriental rugs. Two key figures in the Fieldcrest organization have been Frederic C. Dumaine, a director, and Harold W. Whitcomb, a former president and chairman of the board of directors.

Reidsville Cotton Mill, founded in 1889 by Andrew J. Boyd, who was the first president, was later reorganized as Hermitage Cotton Mill. During the Panic of 1893 the facility was purchased by W. S. Forbes of Richmond, Virginia, who renamed it Edna Mill in honor of his daughter. J. Benton Pipkin joined this company in 1900 and became its president in 1931. His son, W. Benton Pipkin, succeeded to the presidency in 1943 and three years later sold the firm to the Cone textile interests of Greensboro, the present owner.

Three of the county's best-known textile facilities were the Spray Mercantile Company (top), Lily Mill (center), and Reidsville Cotton Mill, later known as Edna Mill (bottom). Photograph at top (ca. 1910) from picture postcard in the possession of the Division of Archives and History; at center courtesy Special Collections, Rockingham Community College Library; at bottom from *Drummond's Pictorial Atlas of North Carolina*, p. 105.

Gem-Dandy of Madison was an outgrowth of the Penn Brothers Suspender Company, which was established in 1914 by Harry, George, and Howard Penn. Green Penn, the son of Harry, later patented an adjustable garter for women; he named this new product the Gem-Dandy and in 1921 established the Gem-Dandy Garter Company. Gem-Dandy has produced a wide range of clothing accessories, particularly garters, suspenders, lingerie, and foundation garments.

Burlington Industries, the largest textile-manufacturing firm in the world, came to Reidsville in 1933 and presently operates a large drapery plant there. Madison Throwing Company, which produces textured yarns, began operations in the former Madison Armory in 1947 and today maintains plants in Madison, Mayodan, and Stoneville.

Other textile companies in the county include Macfield's plants in Madison and Reidsville, which manufacture textured yarns; Brookside Industries in Reidsville, a garment manufacturer; Chase Bag Company, also of Reidsville; and Baxter, Kelly, and Faust of Stoneville, which produces plush fabrics.

The Miller Era

A third major industry became associated with Rockingham County with the long-expected announcement in 1976 by Miller Brewing Company of Milwaukee, a subsidiary of Philip Morris, Inc., that it had acquired 1,700 acres of land adjacent to Eden for the site of a new brewery. During the 1970s Miller, through vigorous growth and aggressive promotion, moved from seventh to second place in the American brewing industry. The new mid-Atlantic brewery at Eden was initially projected to produce beer at the rate of 3 million barrels per year, but during the course of construction the plant was expanded to a capacity of 10 million barrels annually. Construction began in June, 1976, and commercial production commenced in March, 1978. At the present time the plant produces Lowenbrau, Miller High Life, and Lite brand beers. With

Aerial view (1981) of Miller Brewing Company's brewery at Eden, the largest industrial plant in Rockingham County. Photograph courtesy Miller Brewing Company, Eden.

over 1,000 employees, the brewery has made a significant contribution to the economic future of the county, where brewery-related industries have recently located. One notable example is the newly opened Reidsville Can Company, which employs more than 300 people and manufactures containers for Miller.

Tom Price: "The Man Who Matched a Mountain"

Thomas Moore Price (1891-1965) was born near Madison. After receiving an engineering degree at the University of North Carolina in 1915 he worked with a paving contractor. His chance meeting with Henry J. Kaiser in Seattle, Washington, in 1919 set his life's course. Price designed gravel and sand plants for Kaiser, two of which were utilized during construction of Boulder and Grand Coulee dams, and he eventually became an executive vice-president of Kaiser Industries. His major achievement came in the desolate western desert area of Australia, where he explored and made an important discovery of iron ore in the Hammersley Range and was instrumental in planning construction of a railroad to the range. Mount Tom Price, one of the mountains in the Hammersley Range, is regarded as one of the world's richest deposits of iron ore, and the nearby town of Tom Price is a mining community.

The World Wars

The history of Rockingham County's participation in the great world wars of this century has yet to be researched. The tobacco factories and textile mills, of course, made significant contributions to the comfort and morale of the armed forces. Local citizens were involved in Red Cross work and fund raising, and the National Guard units of the Thirtieth Division were called into active service during the Second World War. Robert O. (Opie) Lindsay of Madison, a pilot in the 139th Aero Squadron in France during World War I, was deemed an "ace" (for shooting down five or more enemy planes) and was decorated with the Distinguished Service Cross for downing two German planes on October 18, 1918.

A brief history of the Reidsville National Guard unit, Headquarters Company, 120th Infantry Regiment, chronicles the participation of the unit in the Second World War. After landing in Normandy several days after the D-Day invasion, the Thirtieth Division moved across northern France into Belgium, Holland, and finally Germany. Lieutenant Colonel Paul W. McCollum, a native of Wentworth, was killed in action during the attack on the Siegfried Line in October, 1944. Six men from the original Reidsville unit were killed in the war. A total of 131 men from Rockingham County gave their lives in World War II.

The Great Depression

The county endured hard times during the Great Depression, but there were relatively few industrial, commercial, or banking failures there during that period. The Union Bank and Trust Company of Reidsville failed, and the newly opened Annie Penn Memorial Hospital closed in 1932 but was able to reopen a year later. The textile mills were forced to reduce wages and lay off employees, but public works programs were initiated to help the unemployed. Several important buildings were constructed under federal government relief programs during the Depression: the post offices in Leaksville, Madison, and Reidsville; the county library in Leaksville; the court building in Spray; an addition to the county jail in Wentworth; and National Guard armories in Madison, Reidsville, and Leaksville. Architecturally, the most significant of these structures was the Reidsville post office, rendered in modern Art Déco style and dedicated in 1937 by Postmaster General James A. Farley.

Education

During the early part of the twentieth century, private schools played an important role in secondary education. The trend, however, was toward public education, and four public school systems—Leaksville, Madison, Reidsville, and Rockingham County—ultimately evolved. Consolidation of the many small rural schools and even the one-room schools in the towns began during the 1930s and was completed among the black schools after the Second World War. Two leading black educators who laid a sound foundation for their schools were J. A. McRae of Reidsville and Lawrence E. Boyd, the first principal of Douglas High School in Leaksville.

Two notable private schools at the turn of the century were the Sharp Institute of Intelligence and the Leaksville-Spray Institute. The Sharp Institute, founded by J. M. Sharp, who was later an attorney in Reidsville, opened in 1900 with fifty students but rapidly expanded to over 200. This school offered four courses of study: literary, normal (teacher preparation), business, and music. The Leaksville-Spray Institute, founded in 1904 by local Baptists, opened the following year with nearly a hundred students. Under the leadership of J. H. Beam and later C. M. Beach, the institute offered primary, preparatory, and classical curricula. This school closed in 1918, but the buildings it occupied later became the site of Leaksville High School. The institute's administration-classroom building and the girls' dormitory are presently part of the Eden Intermediate School.

Two important figures in public education in Leaksville were George DeShazo, who was principal of the "little red schoolhouse" of Spray, and the versatile Price H. Gwyn, Presbyterian minister, educator, and banker. Gwyn became principal of Leaksville Graded School in 1911 and

Three of the county's early schools. TOP: Administration building of Leaksville-Spray Institute about 1905, later the site of Leaksville High School; CENTER: a rural school for blacks, erected in 1913 near Sadler; BOTTOM: Stoneville High School, ca. 1930. Photographs courtesy Special Collections, Rockingham Community College.

superintendent of the Leaksville schools in 1918. When the Leaks-ville and Spray schools were combined in the Leaksville Township District in 1921, the first superintendent was James E. Holmes.

The establishment of Rockingham Community College in Wentworth has been the most significant development in the county's educational history in this century. The General Assembly passed the Community College Act in 1963, and the citizens of Rockingham County approved a $1.25 million bond issue to finance construction of the local facility. Welsford Bishopric became chairman of the institution's board of trustees. Dr. Gerald B. James became the first president in 1964, and the college opened in 1966 with a comprehensive educational curriculum encompassing college-transfer, two-year technical, one-year vocational, adult basic, adult high school, and continuing-education programs. At the modern Wentworth campus thousands of people from Rockingham County and the surrounding area have taken courses that have led to college degrees, new or improved job skills, or enrichment of their lives.

The Learning Resources Center at Rockingham Community College, Wentworth. Photograph courtesy Special Collections, Rockingham Community College Library.

The Social Turmoil of the 1960s

In light of events that transpired in many metropolitan areas during the 1960s, Rockingham County experienced little strife. Racial integration of the public schools proceeded without violence during this decade, although tensions that existed in the high schools occasionally resulted in incidents that forced them to close before the end of a school day. All four of the county's school systems were completely desegregated through the redrawing of school districts and the full integration of faculties. As the Vietnam conflict dragged on, the turbulence generated by the antiwar movement in other sections of the nation bypassed the county. A number of Rockingham County men served in various branches of the armed forces with the general support of the hometown folks. In 1972 when Steve Ritchie of Reidsville became the first air force ace of the war, thousands of people turned out in October to honor him on "Steve Ritchie Day."

85

Religion

During the twentieth century the county's churches have grown both in number and in diversity of denomination. The trend of the present century has been for the mainline denominations—Baptist, Methodist, Presbyterian, and Episcopal—to be augmented by a host of others including Wesleyan, Brethren, Pentecostal Holiness, United Church of Christ, Disciples of Christ, Mormon, Friends, Lutheran, Moravian, and many independent Baptists. Two Roman Catholic congregations and churches representing practically every branch of the Protestant faith exist in the county at the present time.

Two of the county's church buildings. LEFT: Mayodan Moravian Church, Mayodan; RIGHT: St. Paul Methodist Church, erected in 1921 and demolished in 1974. This structure once housed a black congregation in Reidsville. Photograph at left (ca. 1919) courtesy Jeff Bullins; at right (ca. 1930) courtesy Treva Nunnally.

Cultural Contributions

Citizens of Rockingham County have made their contributions to literature and the fine arts primarily on the local level. Only in the realm of native bluegrass or country music have residents of Rockingham had a significant influence beyond the county's borders.

Around the turn of the century many mountain families migrated from southern Virginia to the mills in Spray, bringing their music and instruments with them. During the 1920s one of the best-known professional country bands was the North Carolina Ramblers, formed by Charlie Poole, who played the banjo, and Posey Rorer, a fiddler. Other local musicians who played with them were Norman Woodlief and Roy Harvey on guitar and Lonnie Austin on the fiddle. Between 1925 and 1930 the Ramblers made a number of records in New York. They played professionally throughout the region from Spray to Beckley, West Virginia. The music of the Ramblers has been rediscovered in recent years and is being heard not only at home but also in Japan and Great Britain. Both Poole and Rorer are buried in Spray. Another local composer of country music, Lonnie L. Irving of Leaksville, received just prior to his death in 1960 a citation of achievement in country and western music for his best-selling song entitled "Pinball Machine."

Martha Taylor Davison of Leaksville is the only native composer of classical music to achieve statewide and national recognition. She received the North Carolina Federation of Music Clubs's award for the best musical composition in the state in 1937 and in 1943. A performance of her song "O Lawd, Hear My Pray'r" was given at Lake Chautauqua, New York, in 1942. A music club founded in Leaksville in 1938 and named for Mrs. Davison has made a significant contribution to the community.

The literary history of the county encompasses minor local poets and a few novelists. Alexander Martin's eulogy "On the Death of Gov. Caswell" is the earliest poem written by a resident, but the best-known poem is "Hills of Dan" by Abraham F. Morehead (1814-1834). In recent years the works of several local poets—Marjorie Craig, Berta King Ray, and John M. Carter—have been published. Much of the county's poetry has been stimulated by the Fine Arts Festival, which was the dream of Miss Marianne Martin, a former county librarian. The first such festival was held in 1945, and the Fine Arts Association was founded in 1948. Dr. Carl Tyner served as the first president. The Fine Arts Festival spring show, which features art, crafts, and literature, is a popular local event.

Cooleemee, by Annie Eliza Johns (1831-1889), published in 1880, is the first novel written in the county. This romance has little appeal for modern readers, but it does contain passages describing the author's ex-

Annie Eliza Johns of Leaksville, author of the novel *Cooleemee*. Portrait held by Danville, Virginia, chapter of the United Daughters of the Confederacy; photograph supplied by the author.

periences as a nurse in Danville during the Civil War. Peirson Ricks of Mayodan wrote *Hunter's Horn,* a historical novel published in New York in 1947, and Frank A. Clarvoe, who grew up in Mayodan, wrote *The Wonderful Way* (1956), which contains scenes set in the town. The county's most prolific prose writer is Dr. Hugh F. Rankin, a native of Reidsville, professor of history at Tulane University, and a leading scholar of the American Revolution.

The early academies had libraries, but the first true public library in the county was established in Madison by Andrew Betts in 1892 and existed for only a brief time. The present county library system was founded in 1930 when Mrs. Lily M. Mebane of Spray donated her personal library to the community for public use. In 1934 the county commissioners were persuaded to contribute to this collection, and in 1936 the Works Progress Administration constructed a library building. Two years later Miss Marianne Martin was hired as the first county librarian. The present county librarian, Mrs. Martha Davis of Reidsville, presides over one of the finest public library systems for a county of comparable size in the state. New library facilities are presently in Reidsville, Eden, Stoneville, Mayodan, and Madison, and a bookmobile program reaches citizens in the rural areas.

The only art museum in the county is the Chinqua-Penn plantation, the former home of Jeff and Betsy Penn. Mrs. Penn donated her home in 1959 to the Woman's College of the University of North Carolina (presently the University of North Carolina at Greensboro), which has preserved it and opened it to the public. The Penns frequently traveled abroad and brought home a diverse collection of art objects and antiques.

Reidsville's Chinqua-Penn, the former home of Jeff and Betsy Penn, presently serves as a museum and is open to the public. Photograph from *State*, XXXIV (August 1, 1966), p. 13.

Interest in historic preservation has increased considerably in recent years. The Rockingham County Historical Society, founded in 1954, has recently completed restoration of Wright Tavern in Wentworth with local, state, and federal support. The historic structure serves as a headquarters for the society, a restored tavern, and a county museum of history. The tavern was officially dedicated in October, 1980, and is currently open on a limited basis for historical tours. It presently houses the Wentworth post office.

Madison, Reidsville, and Eden have established historical commissions for the purposes of conducting architectural surveys and preserving the physical heritage of the community by establishing historic districts and nominating specific structures for inclusion in the National Register of Historic Places. The Madison survey has been published, and the Madison Historical Commission is currently engaged in restoration of the Governor Alfred M. Scales Law Office. The Reidsville survey was published in 1981, and the city's historical commission has acquired for preservation the Thomas S. Reid house, the last home of Governor David S. Reid. The Eden Preservation Society is beginning its survey and has acquired an antebellum brick house in the Spray area, which it hopes to restore. A county survey is being conducted by members of the historical society, and for future reference the county will have a complete inventory of worthy structures and historic sites that will provide an excellent key to the architectural heritage of the area.

Entertainment

The news media are represented by three local newspapers—the *Eden Daily News*, the *Madison Messenger*, and the *Reidsville Review*—and by the "Rockingham Leader" edition of the *Greensboro Daily News*. WLOE in Eden, founded in 1946 by Doug Craddock, was the first radio station in the county. At the present time Eden has another radio station, WCBX; Reidsville is served by three stations: WKXQ, WREV, and WWMO; and Mayodan is the home of WMYN. The *Advisor*, a county magazine, first appeared in 1941 and has been published continuously since 1946.

About the turn of the century Reidsville boasted a renowned racetrack, vestiges of which still exist. Local interest in sports during this century has revolved around semiprofessional baseball—namely the Tri-City Trips and the Reidsville Luckies—but recently has turned to high school basketball. Intense rivalry among the various schools has led to the emergence of quality teams and nine state championships for county towns. The first world championship won by a resident of the county was awarded in 1981 to fifteen-year-old Jeff Webster of the Shiloh community, who traveled to Bristol, England, to compete successfully for the World Youth Checkers championship.

Motion pictures have been a favorite form of entertainment in the twentieth century. Leaksville once had three theaters for white people— the Colonial, the Grand, and the Boulevard, all of which are gone—and one for blacks. For a time Draper had a theater. Reidsville has had several theaters, including the Grand and the Reid, but only the grandest of them all, the Rockingham, has survived to the present time. Built in 1929 in Spanish mission style, the Rockingham was the region's first theater equipped for sound. It attracted patrons from a wide area.

W. C. (Mutt) Burton, a lifelong resident of Reidsville, newspaper columnist, circus buff, and photographer, is the county's most successful professional actor. In addition to appearing in regional community theater and academic productions, he has had summer engagements with the state theater at Flat Rock, the Parkway Playhouse at Burnsville, and Tanglewood in Forsyth County. He recently made a brief character appearance in the acclaimed film *Being There*.

The Future

Rockingham County has the potential for a bright future. The local economy is soundly based on agriculture and a diversified industrial foundation of tobacco, textiles, and brewing. The county enjoys abundant power and water, good transportation connections, and excellent educational facilities. Typical of North Carolina, Rockingham County's population is evenly divided between rural and urban, with the urban population dispersed rather than concentrated. The air and water are clean; and the land, often occupied by the same families for a century or more, has not been desecrated. Wise planning and preservation of the local heritage will assure that future generations will continue to reap the rewards of living in "so beautiful a dwelling. . . ."

BIBLIOGRAPHICAL ESSAY

Although Rockingham County is nearly two centuries old, a thorough, scholarly history is still unavailable. Consequently, the student of the county's history must turn to primary sources located in the county courthouse or in the North Carolina State Archives. Local history collections held by the various branches of the county public library system and at Rockingham Community College in Wentworth include valuable clipping files, tapes, microfilmed records, and newspapers.

Most of the published material on the county is listed in Lindley S. Butler (comp.), *Rockingham County History: A Bibliography* (Wentworth: Rockingham Community College, 1974; revised editions, 1975, 1978), which is available at the various libraries in the county. The *Journal of Rockingham County History and Genealogy*, published semiannually since 1976 by the Rockingham County Historical Society, is invaluable.

A study of the county should begin with the present volume, supplemented by Lindley S. Butler, *Our Proud Heritage: A Pictorial History of Rockingham County, N.C.* (Bassett, Va.: Bassett Printing Corporation, 1971); Albert R. Newsome, ed., "Twelve North Carolina Counties in 1810-1811," Part IV, *North Carolina Historical Review*, VI (July, 1929), 294-301; *Sketches of the County of Rockingham, N.C.: Its Topography, Geography, Climate, Soil, and Resources, Agricultural and Mineral* (Leaksville: "Gazette" Job Print, 1884); *Rockingham County: Economic and Social* (Raleigh: Edwards and Broughton Printing Co., 1918); and Bettie Sue Gardner, *Here and There in Rockingham County, North Carolina* (Reidsville: Author, 1959), *In Memory of the Confederate Veterans of Rockingham County* (Reidsville: Author, 1961), and *History of Rockingham County, North Carolina* (Reidsville: Author, 1964). Published town histories include Vera W. Dillon, *Avalon: A Brief History of a Fateful Town* (Madison: Author, 1974); Ola Maie Foushee, *Avalon: A North Carolina Town of Joy and Tragedy* (Chapel Hill: Author, 1977); Jean and Charles Rodenbough, *A Heritage to Honor: The Town of Madison, 1818-1968* (Madison: Madison Sesquicentennial Commission, 1968); Ronald W. Williams, *Madison, North Carolina* (Greensboro: Piedmont Press, 1971); Carolyn Pool, *"75 Going on 200": Mayodan, 1899-1974* (Mayodan: Mayodan Diamond Jubilee Committee, 1974); Alberta R. Craig, "Old Wentworth Sketches," *North Carolina Historical Review*, XI (July, 1934), 185-204; and Daniel E. Field, "Leaksville of 'Ye Olden Times,' " edited by Robert W. Carter, Jr., *Journal of Rockingham County History and Genealogy*, V (June, 1980), 1-41.

Architectural surveys currently being conducted in the county's various communities promise to uncover significant information. Published surveys presently include Diane Lea and Claudia Roberts, *An Architectural and Historical Survey of Madison, North Carolina* (Raleigh: Division of Archives and History, 1979), and Laura A. W. Phillips, *Reidsville, North Carolina: An Inventory of Historic & Architectural Resources* (Raleigh: Division of Archives and History and Reidsville Historic Properties Commission, 1981).